ILLUSTRATING BASIC

ILLUSTRATING BASIC

(A SIMPLE PROGRAMMING LANGUAGE)

[Donald Alcock]

ALCOCK SHEARING & PARTNERS

CAMBRIDGE UNIVERSITY PRESS

CAMBRIDGE

LONDON   NEW YORK   MELBOURNE

PUBLISHED BY THE SYNDICS OF THE CAMBRIDGE UNIVERSITY PRESS
THE PITT BUILDING, TRUMPINGTON STREET, CAMBRIDGE CB2 1RP
BENTLEY HOUSE, 200 EUSTON ROAD, LONDON NW1 2DB
32 EAST 57TH STREET, NEW YORK, NY 10022, USA
296 BEACONSFIELD PARADE, MIDDLE PARK, MELBOURNE 3206, AUSTRALIA

FIRST PUBLISHED 1977
REPRINTED 1978
REPRINTED WITH CORRECTIONS 1978

PRINTED IN GREAT BRITAIN AT THE UNIVERSITY PRESS, CAMBRIDGE

LIBRARY OF CONGRESS CATALOGUING IN PUBLICATION DATA

ALCOCK, DONALD, 1930–
    ILLUSTRATING BASIC, A SIMPLE PROGRAMMING LANGUAGE.

    INCLUDES INDEX.
    SUMMARY: PRESENTS A POPULAR COMPUTER LANGUAGE CALLED
BASIC AND EXPLAINS HOW TO WRITE SIMPLE PROGRAMS IN IT.
    1. BASIC (COMPUTER PROGRAM LANGUAGE) [1. BASIC
(COMPUTER PROGRAM LANGUAGE) 2. PROGRAMMING LANGUAGE
(ELECTRONIC COMPUTERS)] I. TITLE.
QA76.73.B3A42   001.6'424   77–4154

ISBN   0 521 21703 2   HARD COVERS
ISBN   0 521 21704 0   LIMP COVERS

To My Sons :

Andrew

AND

GAVIN

CONTENTS

PREFACE

To make a computer do a calculation ∽ however simple∽ you must first describe every step of that calculation in a *LANGUAGE* the computer can understand: this description is called a *PROGRAM* . This book presents a popular and widely available language called *BASIC* and explains how to write simple programs in it .

Although more elegant and powerful languages are favoured by professional programmers *BASIC* is adequate for most non-professionals and excellent for beginners .

BASIC was born in America at Dartmouth College, New Hampshire, in 1964 as a simple computer language for beginners . It proved popular and has been copied and extended by many computer makers, colleges, universities and "time-sharing" services . Now, like English, *BASIC* has *DIALECTS* : a program written in one is unlikely to work on a computer committed to another .

There is soon to be a standard for "minimal basic" by the American National Standards Institute † (A.N.S.I. X3J2), and "specification for standard basic" by Bull, Freeman & Garland has been published by the National Computing Centre, U.K.* (1973). These have not yet had time to encourage everyone to fall into line so the *BASIC* you meet will probably not be standard . I have accepted this as a fact of life, and, in writing this book, kept at my side ELEVEN MANUALS ∽ each defining a different *BASIC* . Four of these versions are available on big computers operated by international "time-sharing" services : the other seven on computers ranging from big to "desk-top" . From these eleven manuals I have tried to discover and point out where *BASICS* commonly differ from one another and recommend ways of avoiding dependence on any one particular version . I have used the word "portable" to describe a *BASIC* program written with independence in mind ∽ and treat the need for portability as an axiom .

> † A.N.S.I. X3J2/76-01 issued for public comment in January 1976
>
> * referred to in the text as "N.C.C. standard basic"

YOU DON'T HAVE TO BE A COMPUTER SCIENTIST TO READ THIS BOOK: IT IS FOR STUDENTS MEETING COMPUTERS FOR THE FIRST TIME; FOR THOSE IN INDUSTRY (PARTICULARLY ENGINEERS) WHO NEVER FORMALLY STUDIED COMPUTING BUT WOULD LIKE TO WRITE SIMPLE COMPUTER PROGRAMS; FOR MANAGERS WHO DO NOT WANT TO WRITE PROGRAMS BUT WOULD LIKE TO KNOW MORE ABOUT A FIELD IN WHICH THEY OFTEN HAVE TO TAKE DECISIONS; AND FOR THOSE WHO CAN ALREADY WRITE IN *BASIC* BUT SEEK A BROADER VIEW OF "PORTABLE" PROGRAMMING AND AN INTRODUCTION TO A FEW PROGRAMMERS' TECHNIQUES LIKE "STATE TABLES" AND "LIST PROCESSING".

THE TEXT OF THE BOOK IS ARRANGED FOR THE MOST PART IN DOUBLE-PAGE SPREADS, EACH DEALING WITH A SINGLE "STATEMENT" OF THE *BASIC* LANGUAGE. BECAUSE SO MANY STATEMENTS ARE INTERDEPENDENT THIS ARRANGEMENT DEMANDS FORWARD REFERENCES NOW AND AGAIN, BUT NOVICES TO COMPUTING MAY IGNORE FORWARD REFERENCES FIRST TIME THROUGH THE BOOK WITHOUT FEAR OF MISSING SOMETHING ESSENTIAL TO UNDERSTANDING THE SUBJECT MATTER.

I RECORD MY DEEP GRATITUDE TO THREE PEOPLE WHO MADE THIS BOOK POSSIBLE: MY WIFE, FAY, WHO SUFFERED GRASS-WIDOWHOOD BUT NEVER CEASED HER WARM ENCOURAGEMENT; MY PARTNER, BRIAN SHEARING, WHO HAS TAUGHT ME SO MUCH ABOUT COMPUTING AND ALLOWED ME TIME OFF WORK TO WRITE THE BOOK; AND CHARLES LANG WHO BELIEVED IN MY IDEAS AND PERSUADED ME TO GIVE THEM FORM.

MY BOOK IS INFORMAL IN LANGUAGE AND UNUSUAL IN PRESENTATION. RATHER THAN WRITE A JUSTIFICATION I WOULD ONLY REMARK THAT A CAREFUL READER MIGHT DIAGNOSE A SEVERE ASTIGMATISM IN MY EYE AND A PERSISTENT SHAKE IN MY HAND.

REIGATE, SURREY, U.K.

Donald Alcock
JANUARY 1977

"BUG" IS COMPUTER JARGON
FOR A MISTAKE. THE BOOK
SHOWS THIS LITTLE BUG
AGAINST ILLUSTRATIONS OF
MISTAKES IN PROGRAMS.

1

COMPONENTS OF THE LANGUAGE

PROBLEM

HOW MANY POTS OF PAINT DO YOU NEED TO PAINT THE ROOF AND WALL OF THIS WATER TANK?

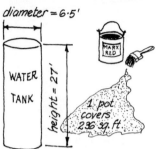

diameter = 6·5'

WATER TANK

height = 27'

1 pot covers 236 sq. ft.

WE COULD GO STRAIGHT AT IT LIKE THIS:

roof area, T = π×6·5² ÷ 4 = 33·2
wall area, S = π×6·5×27 = 551
total area, A = T+S = 584·2
number of pots, G = A÷236 = 2·48
rounding up, R = 3

∴ *you need 3 pots of paint*

OR WE COULD WRITE A *PROGRAM* (IN ENGLISH) TO SOLVE THE PROBLEM.

---

1. **REM**ARK: *A PROGRAM IN ENGLISH*

2. THE FOLLOWING NUMBERS ARE THE **DATA** 6·5, 27, 236

3. **READ** THE DATA, CALLING THEM **D, H & C** RESPECTIVELY
(think of this as putting the data into little boxes labelled D, H & C respectively — see opposite page)

4. WORK OUT 3·14×D²÷4 AND LET THE RESULT BE CALLED **T**
(i.e. put the result in a little box labelled T)

5. WORK OUT 3·14×D×H AND LET THE RESULT BE CALLED **S**

6. ADD **T** TO **S** AND LET THE RESULT BE CALLED **A**

7. WORK OUT **A÷C** AND LET THE RESULT BE CALLED **G**

8. ROUND **G** TO THE NEXT WHOLE NUMBER AND LET THE RESULT BE CALLED **R**
(i.e. add 1 to G and take the integral part of the result)

9. **PRINT** "YOU NEED" ; **R** ; "POTS"
(i.e. print whatever whole number R turns out to be)

10. THE **END**

THIS HAS THE ADVANTAGE OF BEING GOOD FOR ANY SIZE OF TANK AND PAINT POT ⟿ YOU NEED ONLY REPLACE THE DATA ON LINE 2.

 TRY *OBEYING* THE ENGLISH PROGRAM
OPPOSITE & FEEL WHAT IT WOULD BE LIKE
TO *BE* A COMPUTER & *DEFILE* THIS PAGE BY
WRITING NUMBERS IN THE LITTLE BOXES BELOW.

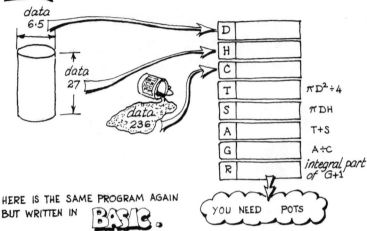

HERE IS THE SAME PROGRAM AGAIN
BUT WRITTEN IN **BASIC**.

COMPARE IT CAREFULLY WITH THE
ENGLISH VERSION OPPOSITE.

```
1    REM    A PROGRAM IN BASIC
2    DATA 6.5, 27, 236
3    READ    D , H , C
4    LET    T = 3.14 * D ↑ 2 / 4
5    LET    S = 3.14 * D * H
6    LET    A = T + S
7    LET    G = A / C
8    LET    R = INT ( G + 1 )
9    PRINT    "YOU NEED"; R ; "POTS"
10   END
```

notice
* meaning multiply
↑ meaning raise to
a power
/ meaning divide

AND THIS, WHEN OBEYED, WOULD PRODUCE :

YOU NEED 3 POTS

3

 PREPARE YOUR PROGRAM BY TYPING INSTRUCTIONS AT THE KEYBOARD ⇌ THE COMPUTER SIMPLY *STORES* THE PROGRAM AT THIS STAGE:

IT DOESN'T OBEY ANY INSTRUCTIONS

```
1 REM  A PROGRAM IN BASIC
2 DATA 6.5, 27, 236
3 READ  D, H , C
4 LET T=3.14*D↑2/4
5 LET S=3.14*D*H
6 LET A=T+S
7 LET G=A/C
8 LET R=INT(G+1)
9 PRINT "YOU NEED";R;"POTS"
10 END
```

TYPE RUN

WHICH SETS THE COMPUTER TO WORK *OBEYING* THE STORED INSTRUCTIONS ONE AFTER THE OTHER ⇌ IN NUMBERED SEQUENCE ⇌ WHILST YOU RELAX.

EVENTUALLY THE COMPUTER WILL OBEY THE INSTRUCTION END. THAT MAKES IT STOP.

```
RUN
YOU NEED 3 POTS
```

 BEFORE YOU CAN TAKE THE FIRST STEP AND START TYPING THE PROGRAM YOU HAVE TO GO THROUGH THE RITUAL OF *SIGNING ON* AND TELLING THE COMPUTER YOU WANT TO USE *BASIC*.

DIFFERENT COMPUTERS ⟨ EVEN IDENTICAL COMPUTERS RUN BY DIFFERENT ORGANISATIONS ⟩ OFTEN HAVE DIFFERENT WAYS OF DOING THESE THINGS, SO IF YOU WANT TO TRY THE PROGRAM NOW GET SOMEONE WHO "KNOWS THE SYSTEM" TO SIGN ON FOR YOU AND CALL UP *BASIC*.

EVERY PROGRAM IN
BASIC HAS TO BE
TYPED ON A KEYBOARD

☞ PROBABLY SOMETHING LIKE THIS ☞

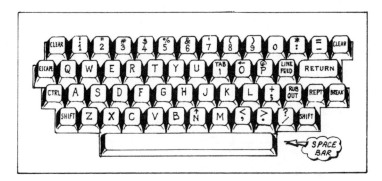

ALTHOUGH POSITIONS OF LETTERS & DIGITS ARE THE SAME ON MOST KEYBOARDS, KEYS LIKE [RUB OUT] & [BREAK] IN THE PICTURE ABOVE VARY IN NAME, POSITION AND FUNCTION FROM ONE INSTALLATION TO ANOTHER.

NOTICE ALL LETTERS ARE CAPITAL LETTERS. NOTICE ALSO THERE IS A KEY FOR 1 AND A KEY FOR ZERO (BOTH IN THE TOP ROW). NEVER PRESS THE LETTERS I AND O IN THEIR PLACE.

AS ON AN ORDINARY TYPEWRITER, PRESSING [SHIFT] AT THE SAME TIME AS ANOTHER KEY GIVES THE CHARACTER SHOWN ON THE UPPER HALF OF THAT KEY: THUS [#/3] TOGETHER WITH [SHIFT] GIVES # WHEREAS [#/3] ALONE, 3.

THE "BACK ARROW" ← SERVES TO DELETE THE CHARACTER ON ITS LEFT FROM THE COMPUTER'S MEMORY: TWO OF THEM DELETE THE PREVIOUS TWO CHARACTERS, AND SO ON. THUS IF YOU TYPE PRIMP←←NT THEN *BASIC* RECEIVES THE WORD PRINT. (REMEMBER THIS BY EXCLAIMING *OH SHIFT!* WHEN YOU HIT THE WRONG KEY.) SOME *BASICS*, HOWEVER, USE AN UNDERSCORE CHARACTER FOR THIS PURPOSE: PRIMP__NT.

MOST *BASICS* USE A KEY (PERHAPS "RUBOUT") WHICH, WHEN PRESSED, DELETES THE WHOLE OF THE LINE YOU ARE TYPING FROM THE COMPUTER'S MEMORY; ANOTHER (PERHAPS "BREAK") STOPS A PROGRAM RUNNING.

FOR A *NEW LINE* IN BASIC PRESS [RETURN] ⟨WHEN TYPING "OFF LINE" PRESS RETURN then LINEFEED⟩

5

 IF YOU INTEND TO USE *BASIC*
A LOT, LEARN TOUCH TYPING.
TEN FINGERS ARE FASTER AND
LESS FRUSTRATING THAN TWO.

THERE IS A LIMIT TO THE LENGTH OF A TYPED LINE ⟶ MOST
BASICS ALLOW LINES UP TO 72 CHARACTERS LONG. SOME
ALLOW LONGER LINES BUT IT IS BEST TO ACCEPT A LIMIT OF 72.

SOME *BASICS* ALLOW GREAT FREEDOM WITH THE SPACE BAR;
SOME DISREGARD SPACES EXCEPT THOSE BETWEEN QUOTATION
MARKS. THUS IT WOULD BE ALLOWABLE TO TYPE:

```
8FORD=STOP
```

INSTEAD OF:

```
8   FOR   D = S   TO   P
```

BUT IT IS OBVIOUSLY SILLY TO OBSCURE THE MEANING OF THE
PROGRAM IN ORDER TO SAVE A FEW TAPS ON THE SPACE BAR.

SOME *BASICS* REFUSE TO ALLOW SPACES WITHIN THE CONTROLLING
WORDS OF THE LANGUAGE. THUS THE FOLLOWING WOULD BE WRONG:

```
23 L E T  A = B+C
```

SOME *BASICS* DEMAND AT LEAST ONE SPACE BEFORE EACH
CONTROLLING WORD, OR AFTER IT, OR BOTH :

```
20DATA  6.5, 27, 236
80  PRINT"YOU NEED";R;"POTS"
```

SOME *BASICS* REFUSE TO ACCEPT SPACES WITHIN LINE NUMBERS
BUT DO NOT OBJECT TO THEM INSIDE OTHER NUMBERS:

```
1 000  LET A = 1 000 . 0
1000   LET A = 1000.0
```

> SOME BASICS
> OBJECT TO
> THESE TOO

SOME *BASICS* DO NOT ALLOW SPACES IN FRONT OF LINE NUMBERS:

```
 95 LET  A = B
100 LET  C = D*F + G
```

> SPACES
> OPTIONAL
> HERE

GENERALLY WHEN *ONE* SPACE IS ALLOWED (OR DEMANDED) THEN
SEVERAL ARE ALLOWED. AND GENERALLY A SPACE IS OPTIONAL
ON EITHER SIDE OF THESE ⟹ (, ; * + / − = ↑ > <)
BUT NOT IN 1.5E2 (SEE PAGE 9) NOR BETWEEN > AND = (SEE PAGE 41).

A PROGRAM WHICH ACCEPTS ALL THESE RESTRICTIONS SHOULD BE
ACCEPTABLE TO ANY VERSION OF *BASIC*.

LINE NUMBERS

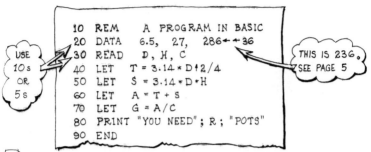

```
10  REM     A PROGRAM IN BASIC
20  DATA    6.5, 27, 286 ← ← 36
30  READ    D, H, C
40  LET     T = 3.14 * D ↑ 2 / 4
50  LET     S = 3.14 * D * H
60  LET     A = T + S
70  LET     G = A / C
80  PRINT "YOU NEED"; R; "POTS"
90  END
```

USE 10 s OR 5 s

THIS IS 236. SEE PAGE 5

THERE IS A *MISTAKE* IN THIS PROGRAM : THE LAST *LET* WAS FORGOTTEN. INSERTING IT IS SIMPLE ; JUST TYPE :

```
75  LET  R = INT (G + 1)
```

AND THE COMPUTER PUTS LINE 75 BETWEEN LINE 70 & LINE 80. IT MAKES NO DIFFERENCE IN WHAT ORDER YOU *TYPE* THE LINES ; THE COMPUTER SORTS THEM INTO ASCENDING ORDER OF LINE NUMBER.

IF YOU TYPE SEVERAL LINES WITH THE *SAME* LINE NUMBER THE COMPUTER OBLITERATES EACH PREVIOUS VERSION THUS ACCEPTING THE LINE TYPED LAST. IF THE LINE TYPED LAST IS *JUST* A LINE NUMBER WITH NOTHING AFTER IT THEN THE *WHOLE LINE VANISHES* FROM THE COMPUTER'S MEMORY ⟿ INCLUDING THE LINE NUMBER. THAT IS HOW TO DELETE UNWANTED LINES. THUS :

```
120  LET  A = B + C
125  LET  E = F
120  LET  A = B + G
125
120  LET  A = B
```

RESULTS IN THE *COMPUTER* REMEMBERING ONLY :

```
120  LET  A = B
```

THE FIRST LINE NUMBER IN A PROGRAM MUST BE GREATER THAN 0. THERE IS ALWAYS A LIMIT TO THE HIGHEST LINE NUMBER : SOME *BASICs* STOP AT 9999, SO IT IS BEST TO ACCEPT THIS AS THE LIMIT.

THE *LAST* STATEMENT OF EVERY PROGRAM MUST BE : **END**
(NO OTHER STATEMENT BUT THE LAST MAY SAY END).

A *BASIC* PROGRAM IS A SEQUENCE OF NUMBERED LINES CALLED *STATEMENTS*.

A STATEMENT MAY SIMPLY *STATE* SOMETHING

```
110 DATA 1, 2, 4
120 END
```

```
30 READ A,B,C
40 LET G = A*B+2 + C
50 PRINT "ANSWER IS"; G
```

OR IT MAY *INSTRUCT* THE COMPUTER TO *DO* SOMETHING. A COMMON SYNONYM FOR *STATEMENT* IS *INSTRUCTION*;

THE STATEMENTS THAT *DO* THINGS ARE *EXECUTABLE* INSTRUCTIONS.

THE COMPUTER FINDS OUT WHAT IS STATED OR WHAT TO DO BY LOOKING AT THE FIRST WORD : DATA, END, READ, LET *etc.*

OR SOMETIMES AT THE FIRST *TWO* WORDS : MAT READ, MAT PRINT *etc.* (WE MEET MAT ON PAGE 76).

BUT THERE IS AN IMPORTANT EXCEPTION :

THE WORD  MAY BE *OMITTED* IN MOST VERSIONS OF *BASIC*.

```
40   G = A*B+2 + C
```

REM STANDS FOR *REMARK*.
REM STATEMENTS CAUSE NO ACTION BY THE COMPUTER; YOU INCLUDE THEM TO CLARIFY YOUR PROGRAM.

```
10 REM        *** WATER TANKS ***
20 REM
30 REM    A PROGRAM TO ILLUSTRATE BASIC
40 REM    -*-*-*-*- * -*-*-*-*-*-*-*-*-
50 DATA   6.5,    27,    236
60 REM    DIAM, HEIGHT, COVERAGE
```

REM FOR BLANK LINES

REM FOR EMBELLISHMENT

REM FOR CLARITY

THE EXAMPLES IN THIS BOOK DO NOT HAVE MANY "REM" STATEMENTS BECAUSE I HAVE ANNOTATED PROGRAMS WITH LITTLE ARROWS AND CLOUDS SO AS TO SAVE SPACE.

YOU CAN TYPE NUMBERS THREE WAYS ☞ AS *INTEGERS*, AS *REALS* OR IN *E-FORM*.

INTEGER FORM
((WHOLE NUMBERS))

160 DATA   0, 2, +4, 1000, -30

REAL FORM
((DECIMAL NUMBERS))

170 DATA +0.70, 4., .6, -1.3, 987.65

(4. MEANS 4.0)

E-FORM
((EXPONENT FORM))
WHERE *E* SAYS:
"TIMES TEN TO THE..."

190 DATA 1E3, 13.6E-4, -13.6E6, -.0136E9

1.0×10^3
$= 1,000$

13.6×10^{-4}
$= 0.00136$

-13.6×10^6
$= -13,600,000$

$-.0136 \times 10^9$
$= -13600000$

E INTRODUCES AN *INTEGER* SAYING HOW MANY PLACES TO SHIFT THE DECIMAL POINT. SHIFT TO THE RIGHT IF THE INTEGER IS POSITIVE ; OTHERWISE LEFT.

190 DATA   E3, 13.6E1.2, 13.6 E 2

IN THE *E* FORM THERE MUST ALWAYS BE A NUMBER IN FRONT OF THE *E* AND AN *INTEGER* AFTER IT. SOME *BASICS* ALLOW SPACES WITHIN AN *E* FORM BUT IT IS BEST NOT TO HAVE THEM.

$\pm 10^{38}$ IN SOME *BASICS* THE BIGGEST NUMBER THAT CAN BE STORED IS APPROXIMATELY $\pm 10^{38}$ ((*BIG* MEANS FAR FROM ZERO ON EITHER SIDE ; *SMALL* MEANS CLOSE TO ZERO ON EITHER SIDE)). OTHER *BASICS* CAN HANDLE MUCH BIGGER NUMBERS THAN $\pm 10^{38}$; IT DEPENDS ON THE COMPUTER'S "WORD LENGTH" AND WHETHER THE "WORDS" ARE USED SINGLY, IN PAIRS, OR IN MULTIPLES. BUT *NO BASIC* SHOULD REFUSE TO HANDLE A NUMBER AS BIG AS $\pm 100,000,000,000,000,000,000,000,000,000,000,000,000$.

6~7 SIG. FIG. IN SOME *BASICS* THE PRECISION OF STORAGE AND ARITHMETIC IS BETWEEN 6 AND 7 SIGNIFICANT DECIMAL DIGITS ☞ 987,654,321 WOULD BE STORED AS APPROXIMATELY 987,654,000. OTHER *BASICS* OFFER MUCH HIGHER PRECISION, 15 SIGNIFICANT FIGURES BEING TYPICAL. AGAIN IT DEPENDS ON THE COMPUTER'S "WORD LENGTH" AND HOW THE "WORDS" ARE USED. BUT *NO BASIC* SHOULD WORK TO LESS PRECISION THAN 6 TO 7 SIG. FIGS. ((THE VAGUENESS OF "6 TO 7" IS BECAUSE MOST COMPUTERS USE BINARY ARITHMETIC, NOT DECIMAL. A MORE PRECISE RENDERING WOULD BE "24 BINARY DIGITS FOR POSITIVE NUMBERS; 23 FOR NEGATIVE ; OR VICE VERSA" BUT THESE IMPLICATIONS NEED NOT BOTHER THE NOVICE TO *BASIC*.))

9

VARIABLES

THERE ARE 286 *SIMPLE* NUMERICAL VARIABLES IN *BASIC*.

WE SAW SOME OF THESE ON PAGE 3. THEY ARE THE LITTLE BOXES USED TO HOLD NUMBERS.

THE FULL 286 ARE SHOWN BELOW. IT IS USEFUL TO KEEP A LARGE-SCALE CHART LIKE THIS AND MAKE A PHOTOCOPY FOR EACH NEW PROGRAM. AS YOU USE EACH VARIABLE WRITE A NOTE IN ITS BOX SAYING WHAT YOU USE IT FOR. THIS STOPS YOU USING VARIABLES ALREADY USED FOR SOMETHING ELSE ⟿ A COMMON SOURCE OF TROUBLE.

	0	1	2	3	4	5	6	7	8	9
A	A_0	A_1	A_2	A_3	A_4	A_5	A_6	A_7	A_8	A_9
B	B_0	B_1	B_2	B_3	B_4	B_5	B_6	B_7	B_8	B_9
C	C_0	C_1	C_2	C_3	C_4	C_5	C_6	C_7	C_8	C_9
D	D_0	D_1	D_2	D_3	D_4	D_5	D_6	D_7	D_8	D_9
E	E_0	E_1	E_2	E_3	E_4	E_5	E_6	E_7	E_8	E_9
F	F_0	F_1	F_2	F_3	F_4	F_5	F_6	F_7	F_8	F_9
G	G_0	G_1	G_2	G_3	G_4	G_5	G_6	G_7	G_8	G_9
H	H_0	H_1	H_2	H_3	H_4	H_5	H_6	H_7	H_8	H_9
I	I_0	I_1	I_2	I_3	I_4	I_5	I_6	I_7	I_8	I_9
J	J_0	J_1	J_2	J_3	J_4	J_5	J_6	J_7	J_8	J_9
K	K_0	K_1	K_2	K_3	K_4	K_5	K_6	K_7	K_8	K_9
L	L_0	L_1	L_2	L_3	L_4	L_5	L_6	L_7	L_8	L_9
M	M_0	M_1	M_2	M_3	M_4	M_5	M_6	M_7	M_8	M_9
N	N_0	N_1	N_2	N_3	N_4	N_5	N_6	N_7	N_8	N_9
O	O_0	O_1	O_2	O_3	O_4	O_5	O_6	O_7	O_8	O_9
P	P_0	P_1	P_2	P_3	P_4	P_5	P_6	P_7	P_8	P_9
Q	Q_0	Q_1	Q_2	Q_3	Q_4	Q_5	Q_6	Q_7	Q_8	Q_9
R	R_0	R_1	R_2	R_3	R_4	R_5	R_6	R_7	R_8	R_9
S	S_0	S_1	S_2	S_3	S_4	S_5	S_6	S_7	S_8	S_9
T	T_0	T_1	T_2	T_3	T_4	T_5	T_6	T_7	T_8	T_9
U	U_0	U_1	U_2	U_3	U_4	U_5	U_6	U_7	U_8	U_9
V	V_0	V_1	V_2	V_3	V_4	V_5	V_6	V_7	V_8	V_9
W	W_0	W_1	W_2	W_3	W_4	W_5	W_6	W_7	W_8	W_9
X	X_0	X_1	X_2	X_3	X_4	X_5	X_6	X_7	X_8	X_9
Y	Y_0	Y_1	Y_2	Y_3	Y_4	Y_5	Y_6	Y_7	Y_8	Y_9
Z	Z_0	Z_1	Z_2	Z_3	Z_4	Z_5	Z_6	Z_7	Z_8	Z_9

PUTTING A NUMBER INTO A VARIABLE SIMPLY REPLACES THE ONE
ALREADY THERE. COMPARE THE FOLLOWING TWO PROGRAMS;
THE FIRST IS THE ONE ON PAGE 3 WITH NEW LINE NUMBERS:

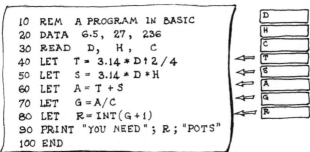

```
10  REM   A PROGRAM IN BASIC
20  DATA  6.5, 27, 236
30  READ  D,  H,  C
40  LET   T = 3.14 * D↑2 / 4
50  LET   S = 3.14 * D * H
60  LET   A = T + S
70  LET   G = A / C
80  LET   R = INT(G + 1)
90  PRINT "YOU NEED"; R; "POTS"
100 END
```

THE SECOND DOES THE SAME JOB BUT USES VARIABLE T OVER AND
OVER AGAIN:

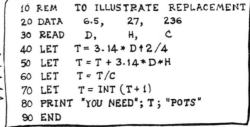

```
10  REM   TO ILLUSTRATE REPLACEMENT
20  DATA  6.5,    27,    236
30  READ  D,    H,    C
40  LET   T = 3.14 * D↑2 / 4
50  LET   T = T + 3.14 * D * H
60  LET   T = T / C
70  LET   T = INT (T + 1)
80  PRINT "YOU NEED"; T; "POTS"
90  END
```

WHEN A PROGRAM STARTS RUNNING EVERY VARIABLE HAS SOME
INITIAL VALUE; IT DEPENDS ON THE VERSION OF *BASIC* WHAT THAT
VALUE IS. IN SOME *BASICS* IT IS **ZERO**; IN SOME IT IS
WHATEVER THE PREVIOUS PROGRAM LEFT BEHIND; IN OTHERS IT IS A
SPECIAL SIGNAL TO SAY **VARIABLE NOT SET**. SO IN THE
FOLLOWING COMPLETE PROGRAM:

```
10  PRINT  V
20  END
```

YOU MIGHT GET **O** OR RUBBISH LIKE −123.456 OR A MESSAGE
FROM THE COMPUTER TO SAY IT CANNOT GO ON BECAUSE VARIABLE
V IS NOT SET WHEN FIRST USED.

DON'T RELY ON ANY VARIABLE BEING ZERO WHEN THE
PROGRAM STARTS; SET IT FIRST:

```
10  LET  V = 0
```

BASIC CAN HANDLE *WORDS* AS WELL AS NUMBERS. WE SAW THIS ON PAGE 4.

```
9  PRINT "YOU NEED"; R; "POTS"
10 END
RUN
YOU NEED 3 POTS
```

THE "YOU NEED" AND THE "POTS" ARE CALLED *TEXTS* IN THIS BOOK. OTHER TERMS IN THE JARGON ARE: *STRING*; *LITERAL STRING*; *ALPHAMERIC STRING*; *ALPHAMERIC LITERAL*; AND THERE MAY BE MORE.

TEXTS ARE WORDS OR SENTENCES OR ARRANGEMENTS OF CHARACTERS ENCLOSED IN QUOTATION MARKS. BY THIS DEFINITION YOU CAN'T HAVE A TEXT CONTAINING QUOTATION MARKS BECAUSE THE COMPUTER WOULD THINK THEY MARKED THE END OF IT; BUT YOU CAN HAVE APOSTROPHES IN TEXTS:

```
20 PRINT "IT'S EASY"
```

HOWEVER, SOME *BASIC*S ALLOW TEXTS TO BE ENCLOSED BETWEEN APOSTROPHES AS AN OPTION; SUCH TEXTS MAY HAVE QUOTATION MARKS IN THEM BUT NOT APOSTROPHES. OTHER *BASIC*S GET ROUND THE PROBLEM BY TREATING A *PAIR* OF QUOTATION MARKS INSIDE A TEXT AS SIGNIFYING A SINGLE QUOTATION MARK:

```
30 PRINT "SHE SAID ""OOH!"""
```

PRODUCES:

```
SHE SAID "OOH!"
```

BUT IT IS BEST TO AVOID HAVING QUOTATION MARKS IN TEXTS.

SEMICOLONS IN THE "PRINT" STATEMENT MAKE THE COMPUTER ABUT THE THINGS TO BE PRINTED ONE AGAINST THE OTHER; COMMAS WOULD MAKE THE COMPUTER SPREAD THEM OUT ACROSS THE PAGE. ALL THIS IS EXPLAINED FROM PAGE 28 ON, WHERE THE "PRINT" STATEMENT IS EXPLAINED IN DETAIL.

TEXTS IN THE "PRINT" STATEMENT MAY BE OF ANY LENGTH THAT WILL FIT THE LINE BEING TYPED. IF YOU WANT SOMETHING PRINTED RIGHT ACROSS THE OUTPUT PAGE YOU MUST PRINT TWO OR MORE TEXTS; ALL BUT THE LAST HAVING A SEMICOLON AFTER THEM.

```
120 PRINT "------------------------";
130 PRINT "------------------------";
140 PRINT "------------------------"
```

TEXTUAL VARIABLES

IN ADDITION TO THE 286 LITTLE BOXES FOR STORING NUMBERS THERE ARE AT LEAST 26 FOR STORING TEXTS; THESE ARE CALLED *TEXTUAL VARIABLES*. WE HAVE COINED THIS TERM TO BALANCE *NUMERICAL VARIABLE* BUT OTHER TERMS IN THE JARGON ARE; *TEXT VARIABLE*, *STRING VARIABLE* & *LITERAL VARIABLE*.

EVERY *BASIC* HAS A LIMIT TO THE LENGTH OF TEXT THAT CAN BE STORED IN A TEXTUAL VARIABLE; SOME ALLOW AS MANY AS 4095 CHARACTERS; OTHERS AS FEW AS 18 ⇆ A MAXIMUM FOR "PORTABILITY".

1 2 3 4 5 6 7 8 9 10 11 12 13 14 15 16 17 18	1 2 3 4 5 6 7 8 9 10 11 12 13 14 15 16 17 18
A$	N$
B$	O$
C$	P$
D$	Q$
E$	R$
F$	S$
G$	T$
H$	U$
I$	V$
J$	W$ ***
K$	X$
L$	Y$
M$	Z$ ONLY 18 CHARACTERS

SOME *BASICS* HAVE 286 TEXTUAL VARIABLES; A$, A0$, A1$, A2$, *etc. to* Z8$, Z9$.

WHEN THE PROGRAM STARTS, TEXTUAL VARIABLES MAY CONTAIN BLANKS; OR TEXTS LEFT OVER FROM A PREVIOUS PROGRAM; OR SPECIAL SIGNALS TO SAY *VARIABLE UNSET*. AS WITH NUMERICAL VARIABLES (PAGE 10) IT DEPENDS ON THE *BASIC* BEING USED. SET VARIABLES BEFORE READING FROM THEM IF YOU WANT TO WRITE A "PORTABLE" PROGRAM.

TEXTUAL VARIABLES MAY BE SET BY "LET" STATEMENTS;

```
10    LET    W$ = "***"
20    LET    Z$ = "ONLY 18 CHARACTERS STORED"
```

LIMIT TO FIT INTO TEXTUAL VARIABLE

AND PRINTED USING "PRINT" STATEMENTS;

```
30    PRINT    W$; Z$; W$
40    END
RUN
***ONLY 18 CHARACTERS***
```

TEXTUAL VARIABLES MAY ALSO BE SET BY "READ" (PAGE 16) AND BY "INPUT" (PAGE 18). THEY MAY BE COMPARED BY "IF" (PAGE 41).

```
50    IF    I$ = "YES"    THEN    80
60    IF    I$ = W$    THEN    9000
```

INPUT & OUTPUT,
EXPRESSIONS AND FUNCTIONS

 THE DATA STATEMENT PROVIDES RAW NUMBERS AND TEXTS FOR READ STATEMENTS TO FEED ON.

YOU MAY HAVE ANY NUMBER OF DATA STATEMENTS ANYWHERE IN A PROGRAM. BEFORE STARTING WORK THE PROGRAM JOINS THEM TOGETHER TO FORM ONE LONG "QUEUE". THERE IS NOTHING TO *OBEY* IN A DATA STATEMENT, BUT AS THE COMPUTER OBEYS A READ STATEMENT IT PICKS UP AS MANY ITEMS AS IT NEEDS FROM THE FRONT OF THIS QUEUE LEAVING THE REMAINDER FOR SUBSEQUENT READ STATEMENTS.

THE FOLLOWING TWO PROGRAMS BOTH PRODUCE THE RESULT SHOWN AT THE END OF THE SECOND PROGRAM.

```
10 REM      UNBROKEN   QUEUE
20 DATA   "ODDS", 7, -23, -17, "EVENS", -12, 36
30 READ    Q$,  B,  C,  D,    E$,  E,  F
40 PRINT   Q$;  B;  C;  D;    E$;  E;  F
50 END
```

```
10   REM       FRAGMENTED  QUEUE
20   DATA    "ODDS", 7
30   READ    Q$,B,C,D,E$,E,F
40   DATA    -23, -17
50   PRINT   Q$;B;C;D;E$;E;F
60   DATA    "EVENS", -12, 36
70   END
RUN
ODDS 7 -23 -17 EVENS-12   36
```

IT IS UP TO YOU TO PUT NUMBERS AND TEXTS WHERE THEY WILL BE READ BY VARIABLES OF THE RIGHT KIND. THE FOLLOWING PROGRAM WOULD FAIL WHILE READING N. (ONE OR OTHER PAIR SHOULD BE REVERSED.)

```
10   DATA   "ANNO", 1977
20   READ   N, ✳ C$
30   PRINT  N;    C$
40   END
```

SOME *BASICS*, HOWEVER, CREATE SEPARATE QUEUES FOR NUMBERS AND TEXTS ⟿ THIS EXAMPLE WOULD WORK. BUT SEPARATE QUEUES ARE UNUSUAL.

IF THERE ARE MORE "READS" THAN ITEMS THE COMPUTER PRINTS A MESSAGE SAYING IT HAS RUN OUT OF DATA AND STOPS WORK.

```
10 DATA  1.5, 2.5, -3.5, 4
20 READ  A, B
30 READ  C, D, E
40 PRINT A;B;C;D;E
50 END
RUN
* OUT  OF  DATA  AT  LINE  30 *
```

 THE RESTORE STATEMENT BRINGS
YOU BACK TO THE FRONT OF THE
QUEUE OF ITEMS FORMED FROM
ALL THE DATA STATEMENTS.

WHEN THE COMPUTER OBEYS A **READ** STATEMENT IT READS AS MANY
ITEMS AS IT NEEDS FROM THE FRONT OF THE QUEUE AND LEAVES THE
REMAINDER FOR SUBSEQUENT **READ** STATEMENTS. BUT IT DOESN'T
DESTROY THE QUEUE. INDEED ON MEETING A **RESTORE**
STATEMENT THE COMPUTER JUMPS BACK TO THE VERY FRONT OF
THE QUEUE AND OBEYS THE NEXT **READ** STATEMENT FROM THERE.

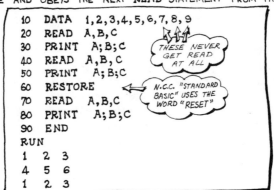

```
10      DATA    1,2,3,4,5,6,7,8,9
20      READ    A,B,C
30      PRINT   A;B;C               THESE NEVER
40      READ    A,B,C               GET READ
50      PRINT   A;B;C               AT ALL
60      RESTORE         ⟵      N.C.C. "STANDARD
70      READ    A,B,C              BASIC" USES THE
80      PRINT   A;B;C              WORD "RESET"
90      END
RUN
1   2   3
4   5   6
1   2   3
```

 ITEMS IN DATA STATEMENTS MAY BE *NUMBERS*
(WITH OR WITHOUT + & − SIGNS), OR *TEXTS*,
OR BOTH; BUT NOT *EXPRESSIONS* (SEE PAGE 20).

```
10      REM     NUMBERS AND TEXTS ALLOWED
20      DATA    1.5, +16.28, −13.47, "YES", "NO"
30      REM     EXPRESSIONS FORBIDDEN
40      DATA    3.14*6.5↑2/4
```

ITEMS MUST BE SEPARATED FROM EACH OTHER BY COMMAS. THERE IS NO
COMMA AT THE END OF EACH LIST.

IF A TEXT IS TOO LONG FOR THE VARIABLE THEN THE EXTRA CHARACTERS ARE
LOST :

```
10      DATA    "FAR TOO LONG FOR THE VARIABLE"
20      READ    V$
                        THE LAST CHARACTER        SEE
                        STORED IN V$              PAGE 13
```

IN THE ORIGINAL *DARTMOUTH BASIC* THE ONLY WAY TO GET DATA INTO A
PROGRAM WAS BY THE **DATA** STATEMENT. MOST *BASICS* TODAY HAVE
THE MORE POPULAR **INPUT** STATEMENT AS WELL. THE **INPUT**
STATEMENT IS EXPLAINED OVERLEAF.

 YOU CAN MAKE A *BASIC* PROGRAM ASK
FOR DATA ₹ IT RESTS IN SUSPENSE
WHILST YOU TYPE A LINE.

```
10    REM     ILLUSTRATING INPUT
20    PRINT   "TYPE ME A NUMBER"
30    INPUT   X
40    PRINT   "YOU JUST TYPED"; X
50    END
RUN
TYPE ME A NUMBER
?
```

THE PROGRAM IS RESTING AT STATEMENT 30 WAITING FOR DATA.
IT WILL WAIT INDEFINITELY UNTIL YOU TYPE SOME DATA AND PRESS
THE ⬭RETURN⬭ KEY. ❨ SOME *BASICS* MAY SHUT DOWN AFTER
A WHILE IF THEY GET NO RESPONSE. ❩

```
? 6·5
YOU JUST TYPED 6.5
```

THE INPUT STATEMENT MAY NEED MORE THAN ONE NUMBER ₹

| 30 INPUT X, Y, Z | ⟹ | ? 6.5, 7.5, 8.5 |

IT CAN INPUT TEXTS AS WELL ₹

| 40 INPUT A$, B$ | ⟹ | ? "REVELATIONS", "THE APOCRYPHA" |

AND A MIXTURE OF NUMBERS & TEXTS ₹

| 30 INPUT T$, C, V | ⟹ | ? "ROMANS", 15, 4·2 |

BUT WHATEVER THE INPUT STATEMENT NEEDS, THE MANNER OF
ASKING ❨ CALLED THE PROMPT ❩ IS THE SAME ₹ IN SOME
BASICS JUST A RING ON THE BELL ₹ IN OTHERS A QUESTION MARK ₹
IN OTHERS AN ARROW OR "GREATER THAN" SIGN.

| 🎼 | ? | > |

SO TO HELP THE USER OF A PROGRAM ❨ WHO MAY NOT BE ITS
AUTHOR ❩ YOU SHOULD PRECEDE EVERY INPUT STATEMENT WITH
AN EXPLANATORY PRINT STATEMENT ₹

```
25    PRINT "TYPE A TEXT & A NUMBER"
30    INPUT T$, C
```

WHEN VARIABLES HAVE SUBSCRIPTS ❨ SEE PAGE 64.❩ YOU MAY INPUT & USE
THEIR VALUES FROM LEFT TO RIGHT : *e.g.* INPUT I,J,A(I,J) .

18

WHAT HAPPENS IF YOU TYPE SOMETHING WRONG IN RESPONSE TO A PROMPT? UNFORTUNATELY THERE ARE DIFFERENT ACTIONS BY DIFFERENT *BASICS*.

TOO MUCH DATA: YOU ARE ASKED TO RETYPE THE WHOLE LINE.

```
10 INPUT A, B, C
```
⟹
```
? 10, 20, 30, 40, 50 ✳
TOO MUCH DATA; RETYPE LINE
?
```

BUT SOME *BASICS* JUST *IGNORE* THE EXTRA NUMBERS; OTHERS *SAVE* THEM FOR THE NEXT INPUT STATEMENT — OR DO SO ONLY IF THE LINE OF DATA ENDS WITH A COMMA.

NOT ENOUGH DATA: YOU ARE ASKED TO RETYPE THE WHOLE LINE.

```
20   INPUT A,B,C,D,E
```
⟹
```
? 10 ✳
NOT ENOUGH DATA; RETYPE LINE
?
```

BUT SOME *BASICS* SIMPLY CONTINUE PROMPTING UNTIL THEY HAVE ENOUGH DATA.

MISMATCHING: YOU ARE ASKED TO RETYPE THE WHOLE LINE.

```
30 INPUT T$,C,V
```
⟹
```
? "ROMANS", 15, "SIX"
WRONG KIND OF DATA; RETYPE LINE
?
```

BUT SOME *BASICS* WOULD ACCEPT THE FIRST TWO ITEMS ABOVE AND RE-PROMPT ONLY FOR THE THIRD; SOME *BASICS* WOULD STOP THE PROGRAM ALTOGETHER.

TEXTS: IF A TEXT HAS NO SPACES IN IT THEN YOU ARE ALLOWED TO LEAVE OUT THE QUOTATION MARKS:

```
40 INPUT T$, C
```
⟹
```
? ROMANS, 15
```

BUT SOME *BASICS* DO NOT ALLOW THIS; SOME WOULD EVEN STOP THE RUN.
IF A TEXT IS TOO LONG FOR THE VARIABLE THEN YOU ARE ASKED TO RETYPE THE WHOLE LINE:

```
50 INPUT T$, C
```
⟹
```
? "THE GOSPEL ACCORDING TO ST. JOHN ",2 ✳
TEXT TOO LONG; RETYPE LINE
?
```

BUT SOME *BASICS* WOULD SIMPLY TRUNCATE THE OVER-LONG TEXT.
SOME *BASICS* ALLOW TEXTS ENCLOSED WITHIN APOSTROPHES; SEE PAGE 12.

COMMAS & SPACES: THE TYPED LIST SHOULD HAVE COMMAS BETWEEN ITEMS AND NO SPACES INSIDE ITEMS. SOME *BASICS* PERMIT COMMAS TO BE OMITTED BUT INSIST ON PROPER SPACING (SEE PAGE 6); OTHERS DISREGARD SPACES (EXCEPT IN TEXTS) BUT INSIST ON THE COMMAS.

19

 YOU CAN WRITE
EXPRESSIONS OF
GREAT COMPLEXITY
IN *BASIC*.

HERE IS AN EXAMPLE OF AN EXPRESSION ⌇ THE PAINTED AREA OF
THE WATER TANK ON PAGE 2.

$$3.14 * D \uparrow 2 / 4 + 3.14 * D * H$$

GIVEN D=6.5, H=27, IF YOU WERE ASKED TO EVALUATE THIS
EXPRESSION YOU WOULD CERTAINLY *NOT* START BY WORKING OUT
4+3.14=7.14 🐛 NOR 2/4=0.5 THEN 0.5+3.14=3.64 🐛
WHY NOT ❓ BECAUSE OF CONVENTIONS WE ALL ACCEPT ⦂

☆ EXPONENTIATION COMES FIRST ⦂ DO $6.5^2 =$ 42.25

☆ THEN MULTIPLICATIONS & DIVISIONS ⦂ DO 3.14×42.25 = 132.665
THEN 132.665 ÷ 4 = 33.1663
THEN 3.14 × 6.5 = 20.4100
THEN 20.4100 × 27 = 551.07

☆ FINALLY ADDITIONS & SUBTRACTIONS ⦂ DO 33.1663+551.07=584.236

AND THAT IS PRECISELY HOW BASIC DOES IT.

HERE IS THE SAME FORMULA EXPRESSED DIFFERENTLY ⦂

$$(3.14 * D * (D/4 + H))$$

YOU MAY "NEST" BRACKETS TO ANY REASONABLE DEPTH. THE
COMPUTER EVALUATES THE EXPRESSION IN THE INNERMOST PAIR OF
BRACKETS AND WORKS OUTWARDS ⌇ PRODUCING THE RESULT YOU
WOULD EXPECT BY THE RULES OF ALGEBRA.

THERE IS NO IMPLIED MULTIPLICATION ⦂ YOU CAN'T DO THIS ⦂

$$3.14 \text{ 🐛} D(D/4 + H)$$

AND YOU MAY NOT PUT TWO OF THESE THINGS ⇨ ↑ / * − +
NEXT TO ONE ANOTHER WITHOUT A BRACKET INTERVENING ⦂

$$3.14 * + D * (+D/+4+H)$$

O.K. A BRACKET INTERVENES

HOW DO YOU EXPRESS 10^{-2} ❓ NOT AS 10↑−2, BUT AS 10↑(−2)
OR 1/(10↑2).

ON TYPING EXPRESSIONS YOU MAY SPACE OUT OR BUNCH UP
AS YOU PLEASE ⦂

| 10 LET A = 3.14 * D↑2 / 4 +3.14*D*H |

RULES FORBIDDING SPACES IN KEYWORDS & LINE NUMBERS
ARE GIVEN ON PAGE 6.

20

CLARIFY EXPRESSIONS BY USING BRACKETS EVEN WHEN NOT STRICTLY NECESSARY.

WHAT IS A/B/C ? MOST *BASICS* TREAT IT AS (A/B)/C BUT SOME AS A/(B/C). (TRY 8/4/2 BOTH WAYS AND SEE THE DIFFERENCE.) ALWAYS USE BRACKETS TO MAKE SURE THE COMPUTER EVALUATES AN AMBIGUOUS EXPRESSION THE WAY YOU INTEND.

A↑B↑C IS ANOTHER AMBIGUOUS EXPRESSION: (A↑B)↑C OR A↑(B↑C) ? AND A^{2M} SHOULD BE EXPRESSED A↑(2*M), NOT A↑2*M.

HERE ARE TWO PROGRAMS ILLUSTRATING EXPRESSIONS.

THE DEFLECTION OF A DIVING BOARD IS GIVEN BY $\dfrac{WL^3}{3EI}$

WHERE:
$I = BD^3/12$
& E IS YOUNG'S MODULUS FOR TIMBER ≈ 2×10^6 lb/sq.in. approx.

```
10  PRINT "TYPE: W(LB), L(FT), B(IN), D(IN)"
20  INPUT          W,  L,  B,  D
30  LET   E = 2000000
40  LET   I = B * D↑3/12
50  LET   V = W*(L*12)↑3/(3*E*I)
60  PRINT "BOARD SAGS"; V; "INCHES"
70  END
```

```
10  PRINT "TYPE: SUM, YEARS, INTEREST%"
20  INPUT          S,    N,    P
30  LET   R = P/100
40  LET   M = S*R*(1+R)↑N/(12*((1+R)↑N-1))
50  PRINT "MONTHLY BURDEN = $"; M
60  PRINT "YOU LOSE $"; M*(12*N)-S
70  END
```

THE MONTHLY REPAYMENT ON A MORTGAGE LOAN OF $S AT P% OVER N YEARS IS:

$$\dfrac{SR(1+R)^N}{12\left[(1+R)^N - 1\right]}$$

WHERE: $R = P \div 100$.

SOME POINTS TO WATCH :

IF YOU WRITE "LET A = B/C" AND "C" TURNS OUT TO BE ZERO (OR SOMETHING VERY VERY SMALL) THE COMPUTER PRINTS A MESSAGE TO SAY "DIVISION BY ZERO" (OR "NUMBER TOO BIG"). IN SUCH CASES SOME *BASICS* THEN SUPPLY A RESULT FOR "A": THE RESULT BEING $\pm 10^{38}$ (OR BIGGER IF THE COMPUTER CAN STORE IT), THE *SIGN* BEING THAT OF THE NUMERATOR OF THE EXPRESSION CAUSING THE TROUBLE. ON THE OTHER HAND SOME *BASICS* STOP THE PROGRAM. OTHER *BASICS* SUPPLY THE BIG VALUE AS DESCRIBED ABOVE BUT DON'T REPORT THE TROUBLE.

—A↑B IN MOST *BASICS* IS TREATED AS —(A↑B). BUT IT IS BEST TO INCLUDE THE BRACKETS TO MAKE SURE.

A↑B IS TAKEN AS 1.0 IF B=0 AND A≥0. THE PROGRAM STOPS IF A<0 ALTHOUGH SOME *BASICS* ALLOW IT WHEN B IS A WHOLE NUMBER.

A↑B GIVES 10^{38} (SEE ABOVE) IF A=0 AND B<0.

 IN ADDITION TO THE
OPERATORS * / + - ↑
BASIC PROVIDES *FUNCTIONS*
SUCH AS *SQUARE ROOT*.

YOU HAVE ALREADY SEEN AN EXAMPLE OF A FUNCTION ON PAGE 3:

```
8  LET   R = INT(G+1)
```

WHERE R ENDS UP AS THE INTEGRAL PART OF THE EXPRESSION
INSIDE THE BRACKETS. THE EXPRESSION G+1 COULD BE MORE
COMPLICATED: HERE IS THE WATER TANK PROGRAM AGAIN:

```
10  PRINT  "TYPE: DIAMETER, HEIGHT, COVERAGE"
20  INPUT       D,        H,       C
30  LET  T = INT(1+(3.14*D*(D/4+H))/C)
40  PRINT "YOU NEED"; T; "POTS"
50  END
```

THE EXPRESSION MAY ITSELF CONTAIN FUNCTIONS: EVEN THE SAME ONE:

```
10  INPUT  X
20  PRINT  SQR(SQR(ABS(X)))
30  END
```

WHICH IS A PROGRAM TO PRINT THE FOURTH ROOT OF THE
POSITIVE VALUE OF A NUMBER.

A FUNCTION IN AN EXPRESSION MAY BE TREATED IN EXACTLY THE
SAME WAY AS A NUMERICAL VARIABLE ⟷ WHEREVER YOU MAY TYPE
X YOU MAY ALSO TYPE INT(X). YOU SHOULD NOT TYPE ANY
SPACES IN THE NAME OF THE FUNCTION NOR BETWEEN THE
NAME AND OPENING BRACKET: HOWEVER, SOME *BASICS* DO
NOT OBJECT TO SUCH SPACES. THE EXPRESSION INSIDE THE
BRACKETS MAY BE SPACED OUT OR BUNCHED UP.

MANY *BASICS* OFFER A GREAT VARIETY OF FUNCTIONS BUT ALL
SHOULD OFFER AT LEAST THE STANDARD ELEVEN DESCRIBED HERE.
THEY ARE CALLED *INTRINSIC* FUNCTIONS BECAUSE THEY ARE PART
OF *BASIC* ITSELF. YOU MAY INVENT OTHER FUNCTIONS WHICH ARE
NOT INTRINSIC AS EXPLAINED ON PAGE 26.

FUNCTIONS   SGN(X), ABS(X), SQR(X), INT(X), LOG(X), EXP(X) ARE
DESCRIBED OPPOSITE: THE TRIGONOMETRICAL FUNCTIONS SIN(X),
COS(X), TAN(X) ARE DESCRIBED ON PAGE 24: PAGE 25 IS
DEVOTED TO THE FUNCTION RND.

SGN(X)
$$= +1 \quad \text{IF } X > 0$$
$$= 0 \quad \text{IF } X = 0$$
$$= -1 \quad \text{IF } X < 0$$
"THE SIGN OF"

```
10 PRINT SGN(7.2); SGN(0); SGN(-.2)
```
⟹ `1 0 -1`

ABS(X)
$$= +X \quad \text{IF } X \geqslant 0$$
$$= -X \quad \text{IF } X < 0$$
"THE ABSOLUTE VALUE OF"

```
20 PRINT ABS(7.2); ABS(0); ABS(-.2)
```
⟹ `7.2 0 0.2`

SQR(X)
$$= \sqrt{X} \quad \text{IF } X \geqslant 0$$
$$= ERROR \text{ IF } X < 0 \quad (\text{BUT SOME BASICS PRODUCE } \sqrt{-X})$$
"THE SQUARE ROOT OF"

```
30 PRINT SQR(16); SQR(0); SQR(-16)
```
⟹
```
4  0
ERROR: SQR(NEGATIVE)
```

INT(X)
"THE INTEGRAL PART OF"
(THE HIGHEST INTEGER LESS THAN OR EQUAL TO X)
(WHERE 0 IS "HIGHER" THAN -1)

```
40 PRINT INT(3.4); INT(-3.4); INT(3)
```
⟹ `3 -4 3`
N.B.

LOG(X)
$$= \log_e(X) \text{ IF } X > 0$$
$$= ERROR \text{ IF } X = 0$$
$$= ERROR \text{ IF } X < 0 \quad (\text{BUT SOME BASICS PRODUCE } \log_e(-X))$$
"THE NATURAL LOGARITHM OF"

```
50 PRINT LOG(1); LOG(10); LOG(2.71828)
```
⟹ `0 2.30258 1`

EXP(X)
$$= \varepsilon^X$$
(where $\varepsilon \doteq 2.71828...$)
"THE NATURAL ANTILOGARITHM OF"
"THE EXPONENTIAL OF"

```
60 PRINT EXP(0); EXP(2.30258); EXP(1)
```
⟹ `1 10 2.71828`

HERE IS A LITTLE PROGRAM TO ILLUSTRATE SGN, ABS & INT.

```
10 PRINT "TYPE A SUM OF MONEY; + OR- "
20 INPUT L
30 LET S = INT(ABS(L)*100+.5)/100
40 LET D = INT(S) * SGN(L)
50 LET C = INT((S-ABS(D))*100)
60 PRINT D; "DOLLARS AND"; C; "CENTS"
70 END
RUN
TYPE A SUM OF MONEY; + OR -
? -123.456
-123 DOLLARS AND 46 CENTS
```

ABS(L) IS POSITIVE WHATEVER THE SIGN OF L; *100 CONVERTS TO CENTS; +.5 ADDS HALF A CENT; INT( ) ROUNDS TO NEAREST CENT; /100 CONVERTS THE FORM TO d.cc FROM THE ORIGINAL ±d.cccc....

D IS THE DOLLARS WITH THE SIGN RESTORED

C IS THE CENTS & IS ALWAYS POSITIVE

23

TRIG. FUNCTIONS

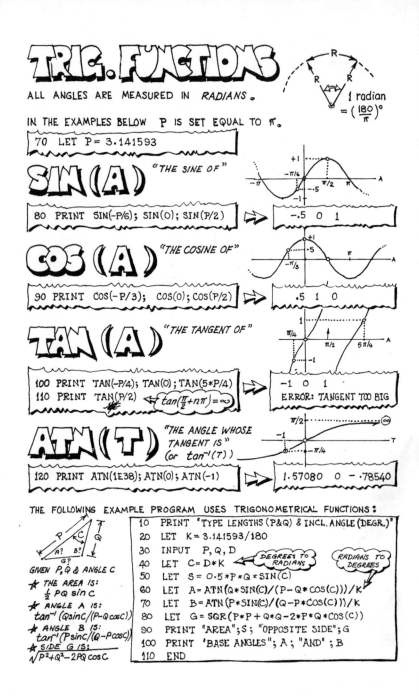

ALL ANGLES ARE MEASURED IN *RADIANS*.

1 radian $= \left(\frac{180}{\pi}\right)°$

IN THE EXAMPLES BELOW P IS SET EQUAL TO π.

```
70 LET P= 3.141593
```

SIN (A) "THE SINE OF"

```
80 PRINT SIN(-P/6); SIN(0); SIN(P/2)
```
⟹ `-.5  0  1`

COS (A) "THE COSINE OF"

```
90 PRINT COS(-P/3); COS(0); COS(P/2)
```
⟹ `.5  1  0`

TAN (A) "THE TANGENT OF"

```
100 PRINT TAN(-P/4); TAN(0); TAN(5*P/4)
110 PRINT TAN(P/2)   tan(π/2 + nπ) = ∞
```
⟹ `-1  0  1`
`ERROR: TANGENT TOO BIG`

ATN (T) "THE ANGLE WHOSE TANGENT IS" (or $\tan^{-1}(T)$)

```
120 PRINT ATN(1E38); ATN(0); ATN(-1)
```
⟹ `1.57080  0  -.78540`

THE FOLLOWING EXAMPLE PROGRAM USES TRIGONOMETRICAL FUNCTIONS:

GIVEN P, Q & ANGLE C

* THE AREA IS:
  $\frac{1}{2}$ PQ sin C
* ANGLE A IS:
  $\tan^{-1}$ (Qsinc/(P-QcosC))
* ANGLE B IS:
  $\tan^{-1}$ (Psinc/(Q-PcosC))
* SIDE G IS:
  $\sqrt{P^2+Q^2-2PQ\cos C}$

```
10  PRINT "TYPE LENGTHS (P&Q) & INCL. ANGLE (DEGR.)"
20  LET K = 3.141593/180
30  INPUT P, Q, D        DEGREES TO RADIANS     RADIANS TO DEGREES
40  LET C = D*K
50  LET S = 0.5*P*Q*SIN(C)
60  LET A = ATN(Q*SIN(C)/(P-Q*COS(C)))/K
70  LET B = ATN(P*SIN(C)/(Q-P*COS(C)))/K
80  LET G = SQR(P*P + Q*Q-2*P*Q*COS(C))
90  PRINT "AREA";S; "OPPOSITE SIDE";G
100 PRINT "BASE ANGLES"; A; "AND"; B
110 END
```

24

 BASIC CAN "THROW DICE" TO GENERATE RANDOM NUMBERS ⇔ PSEUDO RANDOM NUMBERS TO BE MORE PRECISE.

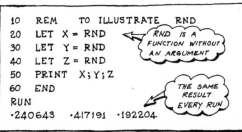

```
10   REM     TO ILLUSTRATE   RND
20   LET  X = RND
30   LET  Y = RND
40   LET  Z = RND
50   PRINT  X ; Y ; Z
60   END
RUN
·240643   ·417191  ·192204
```

RND IS A FUNCTION WITHOUT AN ARGUMENT

THE SAME RESULT EVERY RUN

NOTE:
THE ORIGINAL DARTMOUTH BASIC, & SEVERAL EXISTING ONES, REQUIRE AN ARGUMENT:
LET X = RND(A).
SOME BASICS IGNORE THIS ARGUMENT; OTHERS USE IT IN SUBTLE WAYS SUCH AS TO DENOTE DIFFERENT "STREAMS" OF NUMBERS.

IN AN EXPRESSION "RND" MAY BE TREATED IN EXACTLY THE SAME WAY AS A NUMERICAL VARIABLE; WHEREVER YOU MAY TYPE X YOU MAY ALSO TYPE RND. STATEMENTS 20 TO 50 ABOVE COULD BE COMBINED INTO ONE STATEMENT : | 20 PRINT RND; RND; RND |

WHEN A PROGRAM IS RUNNING, EVERY TIME BASIC MEETS "RND" IT SUPPLIES A RANDOM NUMBER, n, WHERE $0 \le n < 1$ (NB. SOMETIMES 0, NEVER 1). IT IS NOT REALLY RANDOM, IT IS CALLED PSEUDO RANDOM. ON MEETING RND THE COMPUTER GENERATES AND PROVIDES THE NEXT IN A FIXED CYCLE OF NUMBERS. BASICS DIFFER, BUT ONE CYCLE COMMONLY USED HAS A MILLION SIX-DIGIT FRACTIONS FROM 0.000000 TO 0.999999. IN EVERY CYCLE EACH FRACTION OCCURS EXACTLY ONCE. THE CYCLE STARTS AFRESH IN EVERY RUN; IF A PROGRAM USES ALL THE NUMBERS IN THE CYCLE THEN THE CYCLE BEGINS AGAIN. THE PROGRAM ABOVE WOULD GIVE THE SAME RESULT IN EVERY RUN ⇔ BUT A DIFFERENT VERSION OF BASIC MIGHT PRODUCE THREE COMPLETELY DIFFERENT NUMBERS. HOWEVER ...

THIS STATEMENT MAKES BASIC START THE CYCLE AT AN UNPREDICTABLE PLACE ON EACH ENCOUNTER.

THIS PROGRAM THROWS A PAIR OF DICE:

```
10   RANDOMIZE
20   LET  X = INT(1 + 6 * RND)
30   LET  Y = INT(1 + 6 * RND)
40   PRINT  "THROW:"; X ; "AND"; Y
50   END
RUN
THROW:  3 AND 5
```

"RANDOMIZE" ENSURES AN UNPREDICTABLE THROW ON EACH RUN

SOME BASICS DON'T HAVE RANDOMIZE; INSTEAD THEY USE AN ARGUMENT, RND(A). THE WAY "A" IS USED DIFFERS FUNDAMENTALLY FROM BASIC TO BASIC; YOU HAVE TO CONSULT THE SPECIFIC MANUAL.

IN *BASIC* YOU CAN *DEFINE* UP TO 26 OF YOUR OWN FUNCTIONS USING THE DEF STATEMENT. THESE FUNCTIONS ARE NAMED FNA, FNB, FNC *etc.*

COMPARE THESE TWO PROGRAMS, BOTH OF WHICH CALCULATE AND PRINT THE VOLUME OF MATERIAL IN A LENGTH OF PIPE.

```
10    PRINT "TYPE: L, D & I"
20    INPUT          L, D, I
30    LET A1 = 3.141592 * D↑2/4
40    LET A2 = 3.141592 * I↑2/4
50    LET  V = L*(A1 - A2)
60    PRINT "VOLUME IS"; V
70    END
```

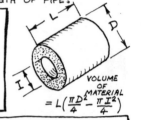

$$= L\left(\frac{\pi D^2}{4} - \frac{\pi I^2}{4}\right)$$

VOLUME OF MATERIAL

"DEF" IS SHORT FOR "DEFINE"

```
10    DEF FNC(X) = 3.141592 * X↑2/4
20    PRINT "TYPE: L, D & I"
30    INPUT          L, D, I
40    LET  V = L*(FNC(D) - FNC(I))
50    PRINT "VOLUME IS"; V
60    END
```

ONCE YOU HAVE DEFINED A FUNCTION (AS IN LINE 10 ABOVE) YOU MAY USE IT EXACTLY AS THOUGH IT WERE AN *INTRINSIC* FUNCTION.

WHAT HAPPENED TO THE VARIABLE X? NOTHING: IT IS CALLED A *DUMMY ARGUMENT*. THIS "DEF" STATEMENT SAYS: "COMPUTE THE VALUE OF WHAT LIES IN BRACKETS; SQUARE IT; MULTIPLY THE SQUARE BY 3.141592; DIVIDE THIS PRODUCT BY 4 ⟿ AND GIVE THE RESULT TO FNC( )". IT WOULD BE JUST AS LOGICAL TO WRITE:

10 DEF FNC(♧) = 3.141592 * ♧ ↑2/4

BUT THERE IS NO SUCH CHARACTER AS ♧ ON THE KEYBOARD SO *BASIC* INSISTS ON THE NAME OF A VARIABLE TO BE USED AS A DUMMY. THE VARIABLE X IS USED ABOVE BUT *BASIC* WILL NOT CHANGE THE VALUE OF X AT STATEMENT 40.

UNFORTUNATELY THERE ARE *BASICS* THAT *WOULD* CHANGE THE VALUE OF X AT STATEMENT 40 ABOVE. YOU CAN TEST YOUR VERSION BY RUNNING THE FOLLOWING PROGRAM.

```
10    REM    TEST FOR DUMMY DUMMIES
20    DEF FNA(T) = T + 2
30    LET T = 0
40    LET A = FNA(3)
50    PRINT T; "SHOULD STAY ZERO"
60    END
```

IF YOUR VERSION PRINTS A 5 THEN YOU WILL HAVE TO KEEP VARIABLES DISTINCT FROM ARGUMENTS: SEE OPPOSITE

YOU MAY ALSO DEFINE FUNCTIONS *WITHOUT* ARGUMENTS ⟿ SEE OPPOSITE.

HERE ARE SOME EXAMPLES OF FUNCTIONS DEFINED:

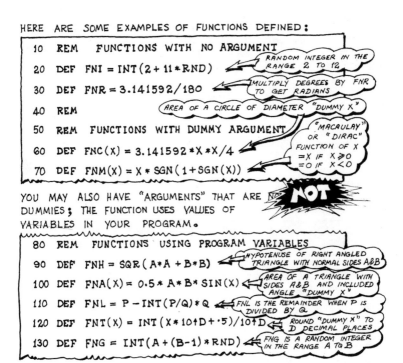

```
10   REM      FUNCTIONS WITH NO ARGUMENT
20   DEF FNI = INT(2 + 11 * RND)          ← RANDOM INTEGER IN THE
                                            RANGE 2 TO 12
30   DEF FNR = 3.141592/180               ← MULTIPLY DEGREES BY FNR
                                            TO GET RADIANS
40   REM            AREA OF A CIRCLE OF DIAMETER "DUMMY X"
50   REM   FUNCTIONS WITH DUMMY ARGUMENT     "MACAULAY"
                                              OR "DIRAC"
60   DEF FNC(X) = 3.141592 * X * X/4         FUNCTION OF X
                                            ← = X IF X ⩾ 0
70   DEF FNM(X) = X * SGN(1 + SGN(X))        = 0 IF X < 0
```

YOU MAY ALSO HAVE "ARGUMENTS" THAT ARE **NOT**
DUMMIES; THE FUNCTION USES VALUES OF
VARIABLES IN YOUR PROGRAM.

```
80   REM    FUNCTIONS USING PROGRAM VARIABLES
90   DEF FNH = SQR(A*A + B*B)        ← HYPOTENUSE OF RIGHT ANGLED
                                       TRIANGLE WITH NORMAL SIDES A & B
100  DEF FNA(X) = 0.5 * A * B * SIN(X) ← AREA OF A TRIANGLE WITH
                                         SIDES A & B AND INCLUDED
                                         ANGLE "DUMMY X"
110  DEF FNL = P - INT(P/Q) * Q      ← FNL IS THE REMAINDER WHEN P IS
                                       DIVIDED BY Q
120  DEF FNT(X) = INT(X * 10↑D + ·5)/10↑D ← ROUND "DUMMY X" TO
                                            D DECIMAL PLACES
130  DEF FNG = INT(A + (B-1) * RND)  ← FNG IS A RANDOM INTEGER
                                       IN THE RANGE A TO B
```

BASICS DIFFER. IF YOU WANT TO WRITE "PORTABLE" PROGRAMS
OBSERVE THE FOLLOWING RULES:

★ MAKE SURE THE DEF STATEMENT IS ON A LOWER-NUMBERED
  LINE THAN THE FIRST USAGE OF THE FUNCTION.

★ MAKE SURE YOUR PROGRAM *OBEYS* THE DEF STATEMENT
  ONCE. (DON'T JUMP ROUND IT WITH "GO TO" ⇒ SEE P.40.)

★ EVEN IF YOUR VERSION ALLOWS IT, DON'T HAVE MORE THAN ONE
  DUMMY ARGUMENT. *e.g.* DON'T HAVE | DEF FNA(A,B,C) = A+B+C |

★ DON'T MAKE FUNCTIONS MORE THAN ONE LINE LONG. SOME
  BASICS ALLOW THIS; YOU SIGNIFY THE END OF A MULTI-
  LINE DEFINITION WITH THE STATEMENT "FNEND".

★ ALWAYS PUT A DUMMY ARGUMENT EVEN IF NOT USED. *e.g.*
  WRITE LINE 30 ABOVE AS DEF FNR(0) = 3.141592/180.
  SOME *BASICS* DON'T ALLOW FUNCTIONS WITHOUT AN ARGUMENT.

★ FOR SAFETY USE LETTER O (ALSO O1, O2, *etc.*) EXCLUSIVELY
  AS DUMMY ARGUMENTS ⇒ NEVER AS VARIABLES; SOME
  BASICS DO NOT TREAT ARGUMENTS AS TRUE DUMMIES. (SEE
  OPPOSITE FOR THIS TEST.)

 THIS IS THE MOST VERSATILE STATEMENT IN *BASIC* AND ALSO ONE WHICH DIFFERS MUCH IN INTERPRETATION FROM ONE *BASIC* TO ANOTHER.

THE FOLLOWING PROGRAM PRINTS THE SQUARE OF ANY NUMBER:

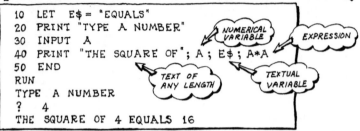

```
10   LET   E$ = "EQUALS"
20   PRINT "TYPE A NUMBER"
30   INPUT  A
40   PRINT "THE SQUARE OF"; A; E$; A*A
50   END
RUN
TYPE  A  NUMBER
?   4
THE  SQUARE  OF  4  EQUALS  16
```

LINE 40 SHOWS EXAMPLES OF FOUR OF THE POSSIBLE THINGS THAT CAN BE PUT IN THE LIST FOLLOWING THE WORD PRINT :

★ "THE SQUARE OF" : A TEXT (ANY LENGTH THAT WILL FIT THE LINE) WHICH GETS PRINTED EXACTLY AS TYPED BUT WITHOUT THE QUOTATION MARKS.

★ A : A NUMERICAL VARIABLE WHOSE *VALUE* GETS PRINTED — NOT ITS NAME.

★ E$: A TEXTUAL VARIABLE WHOSE *TEXT* GETS PRINTED.

★ A*A : AN EXPRESSION WHOSE *VALUE* GETS PRINTED.

A PRINT STATEMENT MAY HAVE ANY MIXTURE OF TEXTS, VARIABLES AND EXPRESSIONS AS LONG AS THE LIST WILL FIT THE LINE. THEY ARE SEPARATED FROM ONE ANOTHER BY *SEMICOLONS* (AS ABOVE) OR BY *COMMAS* WHICH CAUSE *BASIC* TO PRINT ITEMS IN *ZONES* AS DESCRIBED BELOW.

THE PICTURE BELOW SHOWS A PAGE WITH 72 POSITIONS ACROSS IT. *BASIC* DIVIDES THE PAGE INTO 4 ZONES, EACH OF 15 CHARACTER POSITIONS, AND ONE ZONE OF 12. (*BASICS* DIFFER GREATLY HERE BOTH IN WIDTH OF PAGE AND IN WIDTH OF ZONE, BUT THE CONCEPT IS UNIVERSAL.) THE CHARACTER POSITIONS ARE NUMBERED FROM 1, AS DONE BY SOME *BASICS*, BUT MANY *BASICS* NUMBER FROM ZERO (*i.e.* 0 TO 71 INSTEAD OF 1 TO 72).

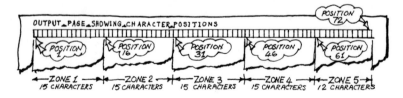

`1 PRINT A; B, C`

A *SEMICOLON* TELLS THE PRINTING HEAD NOT TO MOVE BEFORE PRINTING THE NUMBER OR TEXT SIGNIFIED (IN THIS CASE THE VALUE OF B). IF THERE ISN'T ENOUGH ROOM ON THE LINE THEN THE PRINTING HEAD RETURNS TO START A NEW LINE.

`2 PRINT A; B, C`

A *COMMA* TELLS THE PRINTING HEAD TO MOVE TO THE FIRST POSITION IN THE NEXT AVAILABLE ZONE BEFORE PRINTING THE NUMBER OR TEXT SIGNIFIED (IN THIS CASE THE VALUE OF C). IF THE PRINTING HEAD IS ALREADY SOMEWHERE IN ZONE 5 THEN THE NEXT AVAILABLE ZONE IS ZONE 1 ON THE FOLLOWING LINE.

`3 PRINT A; B,`
`4 PRINT C, D`

THEN WHAT ABOUT THE *FIRST* ITEM IN A LIST (SUCH AS C) ? NO EXCEPTION: *BASIC* ACTS ON THE COMMA OR SEMICOLON AT THE END OF THE *PREVIOUS* LIST, EXACTLY AS THOUGH YOU HAD TYPED (IN THIS CASE):

`3 PRINT A; B, C, D`

`5 PRINT E; F`
`6 PRINT G, H`

WHAT IF THERE IS *NO* COMMA OR SEMICOLON AT THE END OF THE PREVIOUS LIST ~ OR NO PREVIOUS LIST AT ALL ? ANSWER: AFTER OBEYING A PRINT STATEMENT HAVING NO COMMA OR SEMICOLON AT THE END OF ITS LIST THE PRINTING HEAD RETURNS TO START A NEW LINE. YOU MAY ALSO ASSUME THIS HAPPENS BEFORE *BASIC* OBEYS THE VERY FIRST PRINT STATEMENT.

`7 PRINT`

WHAT IF THERE IS AN *EMPTY* LIST ? THEN *BASIC* PRINTS NOTHING ON THE LINE, AND BECAUSE THERE IS NO COMMA OR SEMICOLON THE PRINTING HEAD RETURNS TO START A NEW LINE AS DESCRIBED ABOVE. IN SHORT: *THIS IS THE WAY TO MAKE BASIC PRINT A BLANK LINE.*

`8 PRINT I, "SQD=" I*I`

SOME *BASICS* ALLOW YOU TO LEAVE OUT THE PUNCTUATION ON EITHER SIDE OF A TEXT ~ ASSUMING EITHER A COMMA OR SEMICOLON DEPENDING ON THE PARTICULAR VERSION. DON'T DO IT.

HERE IS AN EXAMPLE SHOWING THE USE OF COMMAS & SEMICOLONS.

```
10   DATA    "DAYS", 28, 30, 31
20   READ    T$,    A, B, C
30   PRINT   "JAN", "FEB", "MAR", "APR"
40   PRINT   , "(29 IN LEAP YEARS)"
50   PRINT   C; T$,  A; T$, C; T$, B; T$
60   END
RUN
JAN           FEB           MAR           APR
              (29 IN LEAP YEARS)
   31 DAYS    28 DAYS    31 DAYS    30 DAYS
```

NOTE THE COMMA AT THE START OF THE LIST, CAUSING A "SKIP" TO THE SECOND ZONE.

PRINT (CONTINUED)

THE SQUARE OF 4 EQUALS 16

AND NOT "THE SQUARE OF 4.00000 EQUALS 16.0000"
(REMEMBERING *BASIC* DOES ARITHMETIC TO AT LEAST 6 FIGURES)?

THE ANSWER IS THAT *BASIC* ASSUMES YOU ARE NOT INTERESTED IN
"TRAILING ZEROS". *BASIC* TAKES OTHER DECISIONS ABOUT THE
WIDTH AND STYLE OF PRINTED NUMBERS AS EXPLAINED BELOW.

IF A NUMBER CAN BE ACCURATELY EXPRESSED AS AN INTEGER
OF SIX DIGITS OR LESS THEN *BASIC* PRINTS IT AS AN *INTEGER*.

```
10 LET A = 654321
20 PRINT  A ; -A
30 PRINT  0.00; 20.0;20.00002
```

SEE THE KEY BELOW FOR ▼ & ▲

▼654321▲ ⁻654321▲

▼0▲ ▼20▲ ▼20

IF A NUMBER IS SMALLER (NEARER TO ZERO) THAN 0.1 *BASIC*
PRINTS IT IN *E-FORM*. MOST *BASICS* PRINT ONE DIGIT
BEFORE THE DECIMAL POINT AND FIVE AFTER, BUT SOME
PRINT ALL SIX DIGITS AFTER THE POINT. THEN MOST *BASICS*
PRINT AN E FOLLOWED BY A PLUS OR MINUS SIGN FOLLOWED
BY TWO DIGITS FOR THE EXPONENT.

```
40 PRINT A/10↑7 ;  -A/10↑9
50 PRINT 0.060 ;  -0.0006
```

▼6.54321E-03▲ ⁻6.54321E-04▲

▼6.00000E+02▲ ⁻6.00000E-04▲

BASIC ALSO PRINTS BIG NUMBERS (10⁶ AND BIGGER) IN *E-FORM*.

```
60 PRINT  100*A ;
70 PRINT  -1000000000 * A
```

▼6.54321E+07▲ ⁻6.54321E+13▲

BASIC PRINTS NUMBERS BETWEEN 0.1 AND 10⁶ IN *DECIMAL FORM*.

```
80 PRINT A/10 ; -A/100
90 PRINT -A/1000 ; A/1000000
```

▼65432.1▲ ⁻6543.21▲

⁻654.321▲ ▼.654321▲

THIS IS WHAT *BASIC* DOES WHEN PRINTING A NUMBER :

- ▼ PRINTS A MINUS SIGN IF THE NUMBER IS
  NEGATIVE, OTHERWISE A SPACE ;
- \# THEN PRINTS AN *INTEGER* OR AN *E-FORM* OR
  A *DECIMAL NUMBER* DEPENDING ON SIZE AND
  PRECISION AS EXPLAINED ABOVE ;
- ▲ THEN PRINTS ONE TRAILING SPACE.

SOME *BASICS* THEN ADD *TWO* OR *ONE* OR *NO* FURTHER TRAILING
SPACES TO MAKE THE TOTAL NUMBER OF PRINTED CHARACTERS A
MULTIPLE OF *THREE* : OTHERS ALWAYS PRINT TWO TRAILING SPACES.

MOST *BASICS* PRINT *TEXTS* AND *TEXTUAL VARIABLES* WITHOUT ADDING TRAILING SPACES AND WITHOUT STRIPPING TRAILING SPACES FROM THE TEXTS THEMSELVES.

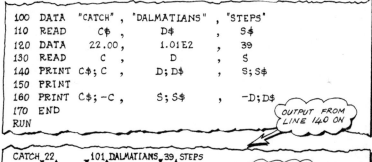

```
100   DATA    "CATCH" ,   "DALMATIANS"  ,   "STEPS"
110   READ      C$ ,         D$         ,    S$
120   DATA     22.00 ,      1.01E2      ,    39
130   READ      C  ,          D         ,    S
140   PRINT  C$; C ,        D; D$       ,   S; S$
150   PRINT
160   PRINT  C$; -C ,       S; S$       ,   -D; D$
170   END
RUN
```

OUTPUT FROM LINE 140 ON

```
CATCH 22     101 DALMATIANS 39 STEPS          ← BLANK LINE

CATCH-22     39 STEPS   -101 DALMATIANS
```

|← ZONE 1 →|← ZONE 2 →|← ZONE 3 →|← ZONE 4 →|← ZONE 5 →|

TYPE AND RUN THE PROGRAM ABOVE (FROM LINE 10 TO LINE 170) TO SEE IF YOUR VERSION OF *BASIC* BEHAVES DIFFERENTLY. FROM VERSIONS THAT MAKE THE LENGTH OF EVERY NUMBER A MULTIPLE OF THREE CHARACTER POSITIONS THE OUTPUT WOULD BE:

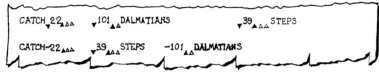

```
CATCH 22        101  DALMATIANS              39   STEPS

CATCH-22        39   STEPS   -101  DALMATIANS
```

31

TAB ( );

MOST *BASICS* HAVE THE TAB FUNCTION WHICH MAY BE USED WITH **PRINT**.

TO VARY THE LAYOUT OF RESULTS *UNDER CONTROL OF A PROGRAM* YOU MAY PUT **TAB** FUNCTIONS *IN* THE LIST THAT FOLLOWS THE WORD **PRINT**.

```
10   PRINT "GIVE ME A VALUE FOR A"
20   INPUT  A
30   PRINT TAB(A); "MAN"; TAB(2*A); "EATING"; TAB(3*A+5);"FISH"
40   END
RUN
GIVE ME A VALUE FOR A
? 3
   MANEATING  FISH
RUN
GIVE ME A VALUE FOR A
? 5
     MAN  EATING    FISH
```

POSITION 5 *POSITION 2×5 = 10* *POSITION 3×5 +5 =20*

A TAB FUNCTION ONLY MAKES SENSE AS AN ITEM IN A LIST AFTER THE WORD **PRINT**. YOU MAY PUT A VARIABLE OR EXPRESSION INSIDE THE BRACKETS ; *BASIC* WORKS OUT ITS VALUE AND MOVES THE PRINTING HEAD TO THE CHARACTER POSITION GIVEN BY THE RESULT. THERE ARE SOME TRICKY POINTS TO WATCH WHEN USING **TAB** :

★ SOME *BASICS* NUMBER CHARACTER POSITIONS FROM 1 (PAGE 28) BUT MANY *BASICS* NUMBER THEM FROM ZERO. YOU CAN MAKE PROGRAMS "PORTABLE" BY ALWAYS NUMBERING FROM 1 AND NEVER USING POSITIONS GREATER THAN 71 .

★ SOME *BASICS* USE THE *NEAREST* INTEGER TO THE RESULT OF THE EXPRESSION WHEREAS MANY *BASICS* TAKE THE *INTEGRAL PART*. IF YOUR FUNCTION COULD YIELD A NON-INTEGRAL RESULT USE **INT** TO *ENSURE* THE RESULT YOU INTEND. *e.g.*   ``; TAB( INT (P/3 + .5) );``

★ SOME *BASICS* DISREGARD THE PUNCTUATION MARK FOLLOWING A TAB( ) e.g. TAB(6); IS TREATED THE SAME WAY AS TAB(6), BUT OTHERS TREAT A COMMA AFTER TAB AS AN ERROR ; YET OTHERS ACT ON SUCH A COMMA BY MOVING THE PRINTING HEAD TO THE NEXT ZONE . SO ALWAYS USE SEMICOLONS AFTER TAB( ); .

★   IF THE PRINTING HEAD HAS ALREADY PASSED THE POSITION EVALUATED BY THE APPROPRIATE TAB FUNCTION ⇒ OR IF THE EVALUATED POSITION IS OFF THE PAGE ⇒ DIFFERENT *BASICS* TAKE DIFFERENT ACTIONS USUALLY RESULTING IN MESSY OUTPUT. DON'T RELY ON SPECIFIC INTERPRETATIONS; GET THE EXPRESSIONS RIGHT.

★   TAB( ) MUST STAND ALONE AS AN ITEM IN THE LIST; IT MAY NOT BE COMBINED IN AN EXPRESSION HOWEVER SIMPLE THE EXPRESSION;

```
100 PRINT   4*TAB(A*6); X
```

TAB( ) IS USEFUL FOR PLOTTING CRUDE GRAPHS ON THE OUTPUT PAGE. FOR AN EXAMPLE OF THIS WE HAVE TO ANTICIPATE PAGE 48 WHICH EXPLAINS WHY STATEMENT 30 BELOW LETS X TAKE SUCCESSIVE VALUES OF 0, 15, 30 *etc. to* 180.

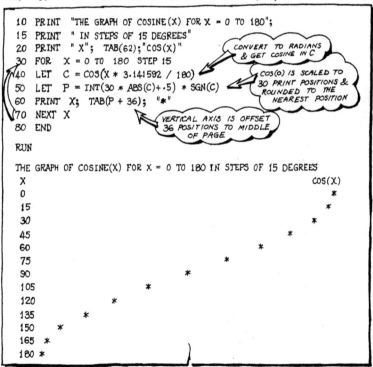

```
10  PRINT  "THE GRAPH OF COSINE(X) FOR X = 0 TO 180";
15  PRINT  " IN STEPS OF 15 DEGREES"
20  PRINT  " X"; TAB(62);"COS(X)"          CONVERT TO RADIANS
30  FOR   X = 0 TO 180 STEP 15             & GET COSINE IN C
40  LET   C = COS(X * 3.141592 / 180)      COS(0) IS SCALED TO
50  LET   P = INT(30 * ABS(C)+.5) * SGN(C)  30 PRINT POSITIONS &
60  PRINT  X; TAB(P + 36);  "*"            ROUNDED TO THE
70  NEXT X                                  NEAREST POSITION
80  END            VERTICAL AXIS IS OFFSET
                   36 POSITIONS TO MIDDLE
RUN                OF PAGE

THE GRAPH OF COSINE(X) FOR X = 0 TO 180 IN STEPS OF 15 DEGREES
 X                                                     COS(X)
 0                                                       *
 15                                                     *
 30                                                   *
 45                                               *
 60                                           *
 75                                       *
 90                                   *
105                               *
120                           *
135                       *
150                   *
165                 *
180               *
```

PRINT USING

NOT EVERY *BASIC* HAS THIS STATEMENT — DETAILED RULES VARY AMONG THOSE THAT DO.

IT IS A DEVICE FOR BUILDING *IMAGES* OF THE DESIRED OUTPUT.

COLON: FOLLOWED BY AN "IMAGE"

ONE BASIC USES % NOT :

```
10 LET G=1000.00
20 PRINT USING 30 ,G, G/20
30:#### GUILDERS! COME, TAKE ##!
40 END
RUN
1000 GUILDERS! COME, TAKE 50!
```

LINE NUMBER OF "IMAGE" TO BE USED

LIST STARTING WITH A COMMA

"MOULD" FOR G

"MOULD" FOR G/20

THE PRINT USING STATEMENT POINTS TO ANOTHER LINE OF THE PROGRAM HOLDING AN *IMAGE* OF WHAT IS TO BE PRINTED. THIS IMAGE MAY CONTAIN *MOULDS* (USUALLY CALLED *FORMATS*). EACH MOULD DETERMINES THE PLACE AND SHAPE OF ITS CORRESPONDING ITEM IN THE PRINT LIST WHEN PRINTED.

AFTER THE WORDS "PRINT USING" TYPE THE NUMBER OF THE LINE OF PROGRAM WHERE THE IMAGE IS TO BE FOUND. (THIS MAY BE ANYWHERE IN THE PROGRAM AND SEVERAL PRINT STATEMENTS MAY USE IT.) THEN TYPE A *COMMA* † WHICH STARTS A LIST OF VARIABLES OR EXPRESSIONS SEPARATED BY *COMMAS*. DON'T TYPE A COMMA AT THE END OF THE LIST; THE PRINTING HEAD RETURNS AUTOMATICALLY TO START A NEW LINE WHEN A PRINT USING STATEMENT HAS BEEN OBEYED. (CONVERSELY THE PRINTING HEAD *DOESN'T* START A NEW LINE *BEFORE* SUCH A STATEMENT IS OBEYED; IT STAYS WHERE IT WAS LEFT BY THE PREVIOUS "PRINT" OR "PRINT USING".)

FOR THE *IMAGE* LINE: TYPE A *COLON* AFTER THE LINE NUMBER. THEN TYPE EXACTLY WHAT YOU WANT THE COMPUTER TO PRINT — BUT REPRESENT EACH *DIGIT* BY # IN ORDER TO FIX A *MOULD* FOR THE SHAPE OF THE PRINTED NUMBER. IF YOU WANT A DECIMAL POINT PRINTED THEN PUT A DECIMAL POINT INSIDE THE MOULD.

```
10:FL ####.##! COME, TAKE FL###.##!
20 PRINT USING 10 , 1000,50
30 END
RUN
FL 1000.00! COME, TAKE FL 50.00!
```

SEE FOOTNOTE

FL IS THE CURRENCY SIGN FOR GUILDERS

† N.C.C. "STANDARD BASIC" SAYS A COLON: IT WOULD BE MUCH NICER THAN A COMMA BUT I HAVE STILL TO FIND A *BASIC* THAT ALLOWS A COLON.

IF THE PROGRAM COMPUTES NUMBERS TOO BIG TO FIT THEIR MOULDS THEN *BASIC* OBJECTS ⟵ SOME *BASICS* BY FILLING THE MOULD WITH ASTERISKS , SOME BY CHANGING OR EXTENDING THE MOULD , SOME BY STOPPING EXECUTION ALTOGETHER .

```
###.##    ⟵ | THIS MOULD CAN COPE WITH POSITIVE NUMBERS
999.99       | AS BIG AS 999.99 AND NEGATIVE NUMBERS
-99.99       | AS BIG AS -99.99
```

NO HARM IS DONE BY MAKING THE MOULDS LONGER THAN STRICTLY NECESSARY.

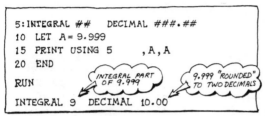

```
5:INTEGRAL ##   DECIMAL ###.##
10 LET A = 9.999
15 PRINT USING 5     , A , A
20 END
RUN
INTEGRAL 9  DECIMAL 10.00
```

INTEGRAL PART OF 9.999

9.999 "ROUNDED" TO TWO DECIMALS

BASIC FILLS INTEGER MOULDS FROM RIGHT TO LEFT: ⟵ ####

BASIC FILLS DECIMAL MOULDS FROM THE POINT OUTWARDS: ⟵ ###.## ⟶

BASIC PUTS THE *INTEGRAL PART* OF A NUMBER INTO AN INTEGER MOULD . *BASIC* *"ROUNDS"* A NUMBER DESTINED FOR A DECIMAL MOULD TO THE NUMBER OF PLACES SIGNIFIED .

IF THE PRINT LIST OFFERS MORE ITEMS THAN THE IMAGE CAN DIGEST THEN *BASIC* USES THE IMAGE AGAIN ⟵ AND AGAIN ⟵ UNTIL THE LIST IS CONSUMED .

```
10  :## BARLEY LOAVES & ## SMALL FISHES
20  PRINT USING 10    ,5,2,10,4,20
30  END

RUN

 5 BARLEY LOAVES &  2 SMALL FISHES
10 BARLEY LOAVES &  4 SMALL FISHES
20 BARLEY LOAVES &
```

THIS EXAMPLE ALSO SHOWS WHAT HAPPENS WHEN THE LIST OFFERS *TOO FEW* ITEMS FOR THE IMAGE . PRINTING STOPS AT THE FIRST FRUSTRATED MOULD .

 THE RULES ARE THE SAME FOR NEARLY ALL VERSIONS OF *BASIC* THAT OFFER PRINT USING.

⟮ AT LEAST ONE , HOWEVER , DEMANDS THE FORMS SHOWN HERE : ⟶ THESE ARE *OPTIONAL* FACILITIES IN SEVERAL *BASICS* **⟯** .

```
100 LET A$="ANS=##.#"
110 PRINT USING A$   , X

100 PRINT USING "ANS=##.#",X
```

THE FACILITIES & RULES OVERLEAF ARE MORE VARIABLE FROM ONE *BASIC* TO ANOTHER THAN THOSE EXPLAINED SO FAR : FOR THE SAKE OF *"PORTABILITY"* IT WOULD BE BEST TO AVOID THOSE OVERLEAF.

PRINT USING (CONTINUED)

 YOU CAN MAKE MOULDS FOR PRINTING NUMBERS IN *E-FORM*
BY ADDING UP-ARROWS TO A DECIMAL MOULD. FOR ANY
ONE VERSION OF *BASIC* THE NUMBER OF ARROWS IS
FIXED : IN SOME FOUR : IN OTHERS FIVE (AND SOME *BASICS*
USE AN EXCLAMATION MARK IN PLACE OF AN ARROW).

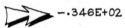

$$-34.5600 \quad \Longrightarrow \quad \#.\#\#\#\uparrow\uparrow\uparrow\uparrow \quad \Longrightarrow \quad -.346E+02$$

THERE MUST BE AT LEAST ONE # BEFORE THE DECIMAL POINT
TO RESERVE A POSITION FOR THE SIGN.

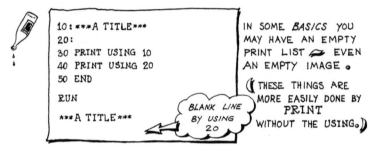

```
10: ***A TITLE***
20:
30 PRINT USING 10
40 PRINT USING 20
50 END

RUN

***A TITLE***
```

BLANK LINE BY USING 20

IN SOME *BASICS* YOU
MAY HAVE AN EMPTY
PRINT LIST ⌇ EVEN
AN EMPTY IMAGE.

(THESE THINGS ARE
MORE EASILY DONE BY
PRINT
WITHOUT THE USING.)

SOME *BASICS* ALLOW CURRENCY SIGNS IN THE MOULD.

$$
\begin{array}{ccc}
1.234 & & \$1.23 \\
23.456 & \Longrightarrow \$\$\$\$.\#\# \Longrightarrow & \$23.46 \\
345.678 & & \$345.68
\end{array}
$$

THE CURRENCY SIGN (POSSIBLY £ IN THE U.K.) "FLOATS" TO
THE LEFT. SOME *BASICS* PERFORM THE SAME TRICK WITH
ASTERISKS.

 SOME *BASICS* ALLOW [†] A PLUS OR MINUS SIGN IN FRONT
OF THE MOULD *e.g.* +##.# AND —#.##

+ SAYS "PRINT A PLUS SIGN IN FRONT OF THE
NUMBER IF IT IS POSITIVE : A MINUS
SIGN IF NEGATIVE"

— SAYS "PRINT A *SPACE* IN FRONT OF THE
NUMBER IF IT IS POSITIVE : A MINUS
SIGN IF NEGATIVE"

IT IS NOT ALWAYS CLEAR FROM THE MANUALS WHETHER THIS
FACILITY CAN BE USED IN CONJUNCTION WITH THE CURRENCY SIGN.

[†] *N.C.C.* "STANDARD BASIC" REQUIRES A SIGN IN FRONT OF THE MOULD.

IN MOST *BASICS* OFFERING PRINT USING IT IS POSSIBLE TO MAKE MOULDS FOR *TEXTUAL* VARIABLES. THESE ARE EXTREMELY USEFUL BUT UNFORTUNATELY THEIR DETAILS DIFFER.

```
10    REM      COMMON START
20    LET   T$= "TO"
30    LET   B$= "BE"
40    PRINT USING 50   ,T$,B$,T$,B$
```

SEE FOUR DIFFERENT LINES 50 BELOW

```
60    REM      COMMON ENDING
70    END

RUN
```

DIFFERENT LINES 50 FOR DIFFERENT VERSIONS OF *BASIC* ARE ILLUSTRATED BELOW. THE RESULT PRODUCED BY USING EACH IMAGE IS SHOWN IMMEDIATELY BELOW THAT IMAGE.

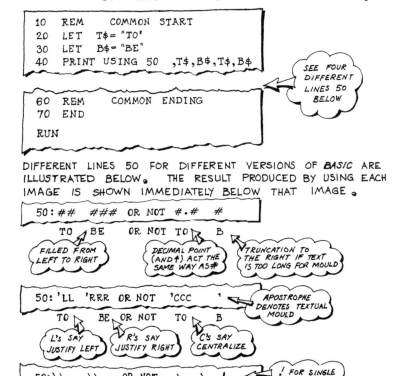

```
50: ##    ###   OR NOT  #.#   #
```
        TO   BE   OR NOT TO   B

FILLED FROM LEFT TO RIGHT

DECIMAL POINT (AND ↑) ACT THE SAME WAY AS #

TRUNCATION TO THE RIGHT IF TEXT IS TOO LONG FOR MOULD

```
50: 'LL  'RRR OR NOT  'CCC     '
```
        TO   BE OR NOT   TO   B

APOSTROPHE DENOTES TEXTUAL MOULD

L's SAY JUSTIFY LEFT

R's SAY JUSTIFY RIGHT

C's SAY CENTRALIZE

```
50: \\    \\    OR NOT  \   \  !
```
        TO   BE   OR NOT   TO   B

! FOR SINGLE CHARACTER

SPACES BETWEEN \ AND \ ARE SIGNIFICANT ≈ THE MOULD IS FILLED FROM LEFT TO RIGHT

```
50: <#     <#   OR NOT  >####    >
```
        TO   BE   OR NOT   TO   B

THIS ONE IS N.C.C. "STANDARD BASIC".

< SAYS JUSTIFY LEFT & TRUNCATE TO THE RIGHT

> SAYS JUSTIFY RIGHT & TRUNCATE TO THE LEFT

SINGLE CHARACTER MOULD — ALSO <

THERE MAY BE MORE WAYS YET. WHY CAN'T WE STANDARDIZE? EVEN BAD STANDARDS WOULD BE BETTER THAN NONE AT ALL.

CONTROL

 WITH THIS INSTRUCTION YOU MAY ALTER THE SEQUENCE IN WHICH *BASIC* OBEYS THE NUMBERED STATEMENTS OF YOUR PROGRAM.

THIS PROGRAM NEVER REACHES ITS END. ON BEING GIVEN A VALUE FOR D IT COMPUTES & PRINTS V, THEN GOES BACK TO LINE 20 TO ASK FOR ANOTHER VALUE FOR D ⌒ AND SO ON ⌒ AND SO ON.

THE WAY TO STOP THIS PROGRAM IS TO PRESS THE ⌐BREAK⌐ KEY

《 OR WHATEVER KEY YOUR OWN INSTALLATION USES FOR THIS 》.

```
10 PRINT   "VOLUMES OF BALLS"
20 PRINT
30 PRINT   "TYPE A DIAMETER"
40 INPUT   D
50 LET     V = 3.141592 * D↑3 /6
60 PRINT   "VOLUME OF BALL IS"; V
70 GO TO   20
80 END

RUN

VOLUMES OF BALLS

TYPE A DIAMETER
?  6.5
VOLUME OF BALL IS  143.793

TYPE A DIAMETER
?
```

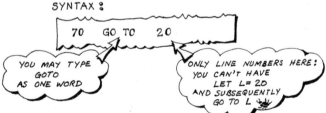

THIS IS NOT A TRIVIAL EXAMPLE. *BASIC* IS VERY USEFUL AS A CALCULATOR FOR EVALUATING FORMULAE FOR SUCCESSIVE VALUES OF VARIABLES TYPED IN, AND THERE IS NO EASIER WAY OF STOPPING THAN PRESSING A SINGLE KEY.

SYNTAX :

```
70   GO TO   20
```

YOU MAY TYPE GOTO AS ONE WORD

ONLY LINE NUMBERS HERE : YOU CAN'T HAVE LET L = 20 AND SUBSEQUENTLY GO TO L

YOU MAY GOTO ANY LINE IN THE PROGRAM 《 EVEN IF IT CONTAINS A NON-EXECUTABLE STATEMENT LIKE REM 》 AND EXECUTION WILL CONTINUE FROM THERE. IF GO TO POINTS TO A NON-EXISTENT LINE NUMBER THEN MOST *BASICS* WILL REFUSE TO START EXECUTION WHEN YOU TYPE RUN 《SIMILARLY FOR IF & ON 》.

IF-THEN

WITH THIS INSTRUCTION YOU MAY ALTER THE ORDINARY SEQUENCE OF EXECUTION ⏤

⏤ BUT ALTER IT *CONDITIONALLY*. THE CONDITIONS ARE:

=	EQUALS
>	IS GREATER THAN
<	IS LESS THAN
>=	IS GREATER THAN OR EQUAL TO
<=	IS LESS THAN OR EQUAL TO
<>	DOES NOT EQUAL

THE LINE HAS TO EXIST

```
20 IF A= B*C THEN 60
```

ONE OF THE SIX POSSIBLE CONDITIONS

> <=

DON'T TYPE A SPACE BETWEEN SYMBOLS IN A CONDITION

GO TO THIS LINE (AND CONTINUE FROM THERE) IF THE CONDITION APPLIES: OTHERWISE JUST CARRY ON

LINE NUMBERS ONLY: YOU CAN'T HAVE "THEN L"

THE THING ON EITHER SIDE OF THE "CONDITION" MAY BE A *NUMBER* OR *EXPRESSION*:

```
30 IF  1+ SQR(A↑2 + B↑2) > 0.2 THEN 10
40 IF     ABS(A−B)   <= 0.01 THEN 15
```

THE WAY TO TEST "APPROXIMATE" EQUALITY OF A & B

OR IT MAY BE A *TEXT* OR A *TEXTUAL VARIABLE* WHEN THE CONDITION IS NO MORE COMPLICATED THAN *EQUALS* OR *DOES NOT EQUAL* (BUT SEE BOTTOM OF PAGE):

```
50 IF  Q$= "YES" THEN  150
60 IF "FINISH" <>  A$  THEN 10
70 IF  R$= T$  THEN 230
```

NOTE: THE TEXTS "YES " AND " YES" ARE NOT EQUAL

IT IS NONSENSE TO COMPARE NUMERICAL VARIABLES WITH TEXTUAL VARIABLES:

```
80 IF  Q$ = Y  THEN 99
```

MANY *BASICS* ALLOW THE WORDS "GO TO" (OR THE WORD "GOTO") IN PLACE OF "THEN" BUT FOR THE SAKE OF PORTABILITY IT IS BEST TO STICK TO "THEN".

MOST *BASICS* ALLOW MORE COMPLICATED COMPARISONS OF TEXTS. GENERALLY "Z" IS CONSIDERED "GREATER" THAN "A" AND "9" IS GREATER THAN "0". A SPACE " " IS LESS THAN ANY LETTER OR DIGIT. THUS YOU MAY SORT NAMES ALPHABETICALLY:

> "A" < "ABALONE" < "ACORN"   &   "V2" < "V8"

 YOU MAY CAUSE *BASIC* TO STOP
EXECUTION AT ANY LINE OF YOUR
PROGRAM USING THIS INSTRUCTION.

THE *LAST* INSTRUCTION OF EVERY PROGRAM MUST BE "END".
NO OTHER STATEMENT BUT THE LAST MAY SAY "END".

"END" SERVES IN A DUAL ROLE:

⭐ IT MARKS THE END OF EVERY PROGRAM FOR THE
CONVENIENCE OF THE *BASIC* SYSTEM WHEN
TRANSLATING *BASIC* LANGUAGE INTO SOME OTHER
COMPUTER CODE STRAIGHT AFTER YOU TYPE "RUN" :

⭐ WHEN "END" IS ACTUALLY *"OBEYED"* DURING
SUBSEQUENT EXECUTION IT MAKES THE COMPUTER
STOP EXECUTING THE PROGRAM.

HOWEVER THERE MIGHT BE SEVERAL PLACES IN A PROGRAM WHERE
YOU WOULD LIKE TO TELL *BASIC* TO STOP EXECUTION. YOU CAN DO
THIS BY A "GO TO" WHICH SENDS CONTROL TO "END" OR YOU
CAN DO IT BY A "STOP" INSTRUCTION. "STOP", UNLIKE "END",
MAY APPEAR MANY TIMES AND ANYWHERE INSIDE A PROGRAM.

```
10  PRINT "DO YOU LIKE PROGRAMMING ? "
20  INPUT  A$
30  IF A$ = "NO"  THEN  70
40  IF A$ = "YES"  THEN  90
50  PRINT "NOT AN UNEQUIVOCAL ANSWER"
60  GO TO  100
70  PRINT "PERSEVERE!  YOU WILL LEARN TO"
80  GO TO  100
90  PRINT "FASCINATING  ISN'T IT?"
100 END
```

THESE TWO SILLY PROGRAMS DO THE SAME JOB AND ILLUSTRATE
THE USE OF "END" AND "STOP".

```
10  PRINT "DO YOU LIKE PROGRAMMING?"
20  INPUT  A$
30  IF A$ = "NO"  THEN  70
40  IF A$ = "YES"  THEN  90
50  PRINT "NOT AN UNEQUIVOCAL ANSWER"
60  STOP
70  PRINT "PERSEVERE! YOU WILL LEARN TO "
80  STOP
90  PRINT "FASCINATING  ISN'T IT?"
100 END
```

 *ILLUSTRATING* GO TO, IF ⟷ THEN & STOP

THIS PROGRAM SOLVES A PAIR OF SIMULTANEOUS EQUATIONS HAVING ANY NUMBER OF RIGHT-HAND SIDES. LET THE TWO EQUATIONS BE:

$$a X + b Y = p$$
$$c X + d Y = q$$

USING CRAMER'S RULE THE SOLUTION MAY BE WRITTEN LIKE THIS:

$$X = \frac{\begin{vmatrix} p & b \\ q & d \end{vmatrix}}{\begin{vmatrix} a & b \\ c & d \end{vmatrix}} \quad, \quad Y = \frac{\begin{vmatrix} a & p \\ c & q \end{vmatrix}}{\begin{vmatrix} a & b \\ c & d \end{vmatrix}}$$

WHERE THE VERTICAL BARS INDICATE *DETERMINANTS* WHICH MAY BE EVALUATED THUS:

$$\begin{vmatrix} a & b \\ c & d \end{vmatrix} = a*d - c*b$$

IF THE DETERMINANT IN THE DENOMINATOR IS ZERO ☾ OR VERY VERY CLOSE TO ZERO ☽ THEN NO SOLUTION IS POSSIBLE.

```
10   PRINT "TWO SIMULTANEOUS EQUATIONS"
20   PRINT "TYPE COEFFICIENTS OF X&Y; FIRST ROW"
30   INPUT A,B
40   PRINT "NOW SECOND ROW"
50   INPUT C,D
60   REM    EVALUATE DENOMINATOR, M
70   LET M = A*D - C*B
80   IF ABS(M) > 0.00001 THEN 110
90   PRINT "SOLUTION IMPOSSIBLE; DET ="; M
100  STOP
110  PRINT "TYPE 2 VALUES FOR R.H. SIDE"
120  INPUT P,Q
130  LET X = (P*D - Q*B)/M
140  LET Y = (A*Q - C*P)/M
150  PRINT "X ="; X ; "Y ="; Y
160  PRINT "ANY MORE R.H.SIDES? YES?"
170  INPUT A$
180  IF A$ = "YES" THEN 110
190  REM   YOU COULD HAVE "STOP" HERE
200  END
```

43

 *ILLUSTRATING* GO TO & IF THEN

HERE IS A PROGRAM DESIGNED TO CALCULATE AREAS OF RECTANGLES, TRIANGLES AND CIRCLES. IT ASKS YOU TO TYPE THE NAME OF A SHAPE ; THEN IT ASKS FOR DIMENSIONS RELEVANT TO THAT SHAPE. IF YOU TYPE ANY NAME OTHER THAN "RECTANGLE", "TRIANGLE" OR "CIRCLE" THE PROGRAM STOPS RUNNING.

THE LOGIC OF THE PROGRAM IS SHOWN BY THE *FLOW CHART* BELOW. THERE ARE NICER WAYS OF ORGANIZING SUCH PROGRAMS USING INSTRUCTIONS NOT YET EXPLAINED ; THIS PROGRAM WAS DESIGNED TO ILLUSTRATE "GO TO" AND "IF THEN".

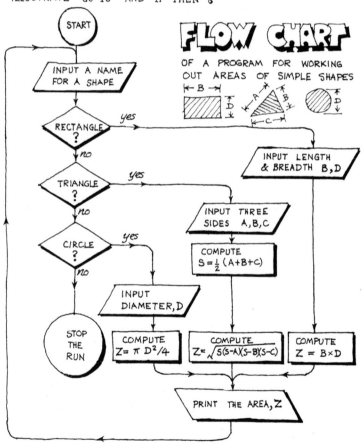

FLOW CHART

OF A PROGRAM FOR WORKING OUT AREAS OF SIMPLE SHAPES

44

```
10    PRINT  "***AREA CALCULATOR***"
20    PRINT
30    PRINT "TYPE: RECTANGLE, TRIANGLE  OR CIRCLE"
40    INPUT   S$
50    REM
60    IF  S$ = "RECTANGLE"  THEN  130
70    IF  S$ = "TRIANGLE"   THEN   180
80    IF  S$ = "CIRCLE"  THEN 240
90    PRINT S$, "MEANS STOP"
100   GO TO  320
110   REM
120   REM
130   PRINT "TYPE BREADTH & DEPTH"
140   INPUT  B, D
150   LET  Z = B*D
160   GO TO  280
170   REM
180   PRINT "TYPE LENGTHS OF 3 SIDES"
190   INPUT  A, B, C
200   LET  S = 0.5*(A+B+C)
210   LET  Z = SQR(S*(S-A)*(S-B)*(S-C))
220   GO TO  280
230   REM
240   PRINT   "TYPE THE DIAMETER"
250   INPUT   D
260   LET  Z = 3.141592*D↑2/4
270   REM
280   REM   FLOWS  MERGE HERE
290   PRINT
300   PRINT "AREA OF "; S$; " IS"; Z
310   GO TO  20
320   END
```

GOES STRAIGHT TO "END"

SPACE   *SPACE*

```
RUN

***AREA CALCULATOR***

TYPE: RECTANGLE, TRIANGLE  OR CIRCLE
? RECTANGLE
TYPE BREADTH & DEPTH
?  14.6  10

AREA OF RECTANGLE IS 146

TYPE: RECTANGLE, TRIANGLE  OR CIRCLE
? NO
NO              MEANS STOP
```

 **ON - GO TO**

THIS INSTRUCTION BREAKS THE ORDINARY SEQUENCE OF OBEYING INSTRUCTIONS

IT IS A MULTI-WAY SWITCH.

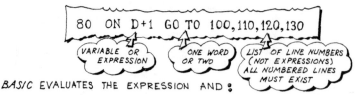

```
80   ON  D+1  GO TO  100,110,120,130
```

VARIABLE OR EXPRESSION

ONE WORD OR TWO

LIST OF LINE NUMBERS (NOT EXPRESSIONS) ALL NUMBERED LINES MUST EXIST

BASIC EVALUATES THE EXPRESSION AND :

- SOME *BASICS* "ROUND" THE RESULT TO THE *NEAREST INTEGER.*

- SOME *BASICS* TAKE THE *INTEGRAL PART.*

IF THE RESULT IS 1 THEN *BASIC* USES THE *FIRST* NUMBER IN THE LIST (GO TO 100). IF THE RESULT IS 2 THEN *BASIC* USES THE *SECOND* NUMBER (GO TO 110) AND SO ON .

```
 10    PRINT    "TYPE A DIGIT FROM 0 TO 3"
 15    PRINT    "PRESS 'BREAK' KEY TO STOP"
 30    INPUT    D
 40    IF  D-INT(D) <> 0  THEN  140
 50    IF  D < 0  THEN  150
 60    IF  D > 3  THEN  150
 65    REM     NOW CERTAIN D IS  0,1,2 OR 3
 70    PRINT    "YOU TYPED ";
 75    REM
 80    ON  D+1  GO TO  100,110,120,130
 85    REM    CAN'T GET HERE
100    PRINT    "ZERO"
105    GO TO  10
110    PRINT    "ONE"
115    GO TO  10
120    PRINT    "TWO"
125    GO TO  10
130    PRINT    "THREE"
135    GO TO  10
140    PRINT    "NON INTEGRAL"
145    GO TO  10
150    PRINT    "OUT OF RANGE"
160    GO TO  10
170    END
```

(CONTINUED OPPOSITE)

46

```
RUN

TYPE A DIGIT FROM 0 TO 3
PRESS 'BREAK' TO STOP
? 0
YOU TYPED ZERO
TYPE A DIGIT FROM 0 TO 3
PRESS 'BREAK' TO STOP
? 6
OUT OF RANGE
TYPE
```

THIS IS A USEFUL INSTRUCTION, BUT BE CAREFUL ABOUT ITS SPECIAL *INTERPRETATIONS* BY DIFFERENT VERSIONS OF *BASIC*.

☆ BECAUSE SOME *BASICS* USE THE *NEAREST* INTEGER AND OTHERS THE *INTEGRAL PART* OF THE EXPRESSION, ENSURE YOUR OWN EXPRESSIONS CAN ONLY YIELD INTEGRAL RESULTS ⟨ SEE LINE 40 OPPOSITE ⟩.

☆ SOME *BASICS* REPORT AN ERROR AND STOP THE RUN IF THE RESULT OF THE EXPRESSION IS OUT OF RANGE. BUT OTHER *BASICS* GO TO THE *FIRST* LINE IN THE LIST IF THE RESULT IS LESS THAN 1 AND TO THE *LAST* IF THE RESULT IS GREATER THAN THE NUMBER OF NUMBERS IN THE LIST. YET OTHER *BASICS* JUMP TO THE LINE FOLLOWING "ON" ⟨ LINE 85 OPPOSITE ⟩ IF THE RESULT IS OUT OF RANGE. SO FOR THE SAKE OF "PORTABILITY" *PUT IN YOUR OWN TESTS FOR RANGE* ⟨ SEE LINES 50 & 60 OPPOSITE ⟩.

BELOW ARE SHOWN OTHER ⟨ LESS COMMON ⟩ FORMS OF THIS INSTRUCTION AS USED IN DIFFERENT VERSIONS OF *BASIC*.

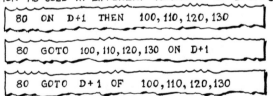

```
80  ON  D+1  THEN  100, 110, 120, 130
```

```
80  GOTO  100, 110, 120, 130  ON  D+1
```

```
80  GOTO  D+1  OF  100, 110, 120, 130
```

THE INSTRUCTION BELOW MAY BECOME UNIVERSAL *IN ADDITION* TO THE "ON ≈ GO TO" DESCRIBED ABOVE. THE MEANING OF "ON ≈ GO SUB" WILL BE CLEAR WHEN YOU REACH PAGE 55.

```
80  ON  D+1  GO SUB  100, 110, 120, 130
```

47

 **FOR—NEXT**

THIS MAKES *BASIC* OBEY A SEQUENCE OF INSTRUCTIONS AGAIN & AGAIN

WE CALL THIS SEQUENCE A *LOOP*.

```
10  LET M = 3
20  READ X$
30  PRINT M; X$
40  LET M = M-1
50  IF M <> 0 THEN 20
60  PRINT "PEAR TREE"
70  DATA "HENS", "DOVES", "PARTRIDGE"
80  END

RUN

   3 HENS
   2 DOVES
   1 PARTRIDGE
PEAR TREE
```

YOU CAN CREATE A LOOP BY SETTING A "COUNTER"
⟨ LET M=3 ⟩
THEN SUCCESSIVELY DEDUCTING 1
⟨ LET M=M-1 ⟩,
TESTING THE REMAINING VALUE
⟨ IF M<>0 ⟩,
AND "LOOPING" BACK
⟨ THEN 20 ⟩
UNTIL THE COUNTER RUNS OUT.

BUT THE SAME RESULT MAY BE ACHIEVED MORE SIMPLY AS SHOWN HERE ⟹

```
10  FOR M = 3 TO 1 STEP -1
20  READ X$
30  PRINT M; X$
40  NEXT M
50  PRINT "PEAR TREE"
60  DATA "HENS", "DOVES", "PARTRIDGE"
70  END
```

THE FORM OF THE INSTRUCTION IS:

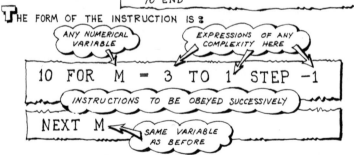

ANY NUMERICAL VARIABLE

EXPRESSIONS OF ANY COMPLEXITY HERE

```
10  FOR M = 3 TO 1 STEP -1
```

INSTRUCTIONS TO BE OBEYED SUCCESSIVELY

```
NEXT M
```

SAME VARIABLE AS BEFORE

IF THE STEP IS +1 THEN YOU MAY SIMPLIFY BY OMITTING " STEP 1 ":

```
100  FOR N = P TO Q
```

LOOPS MAY BE *NESTED* ONE INSIDE THE OTHER.

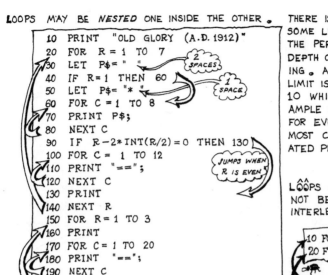

```
10    PRINT  "OLD GLORY (A.D. 1912)"
20    FOR R = 1 TO 7
30    LET P$= " "                    2 SPACES
40    IF R=1 THEN  60                 1 SPACE
50    LET P$= "*"
60    FOR C=1 TO 8
70    PRINT P$;
80    NEXT C
90    IF  R-2*INT(R/2)=0  THEN  130
100   FOR C = 1 TO 12
110   PRINT  "==";                   JUMPS WHEN R IS EVEN
120   NEXT C
130   PRINT
140   NEXT  R
150   FOR R = 1 TO 3
160   PRINT
170   FOR C = 1 TO 20
180   PRINT  "==";
190   NEXT C
200   PRINT
210   NEXT R
220   END
```

TRY IT!

THERE IS ALWAYS SOME LIMIT TO THE PERMISSIBLE DEPTH OF NESTING. A TYPICAL LIMIT IS ABOUT 10 WHICH IS AMPLE DEPTH FOR EVEN THE MOST COMPLICATED PROGRAM.

LÔÔPS MUST NOT BE INTERLEAVED.

```
10 FOR I=
20 FOR K=
GO NEXT I
70 NEXT K
```

YOU MAY *JUMP OUT* OF A LOOP:

† OLDE ENGLISHE FOLKE SONGE "WIDDICOMBE FAIR"

```
10    REM    FIND YOUR PLACE ON THE MARE †
20    DATA "BREWER", "STEWER" , "GURNEY"
30    DATA "DAVEY", "WHIDDON", "HAWK"
40    DATA "COBBLEIGH"
50    PRINT "TYPE YOUR LAST NAME"
60    INPUT  N$
70    FOR  L= 1 TO 7
80    READ  M$
90    IF M$=N$  THEN  130
100   NEXT L
110   PRINT  N$; " IS NOT ON THE MARE"
120   GO TO 140
130   PRINT  N$; " IS NUMBER"; L
140   END
```

THIS IS CALLED *SCANNING A LIST* TO FIND A MATCH.

THE *LOOPING VARIABLE* (L ABOVE) KEEPS ITS VALUE IF YOU JUMP OUT OF A LOOP BEFORE THE LOOP HAS RUN ITS COURSE. BUT IF YOU *DROP OUT AT THE BOTTOM* (IN THIS CASE TO LINE 110) THEN **DON'T** ASSUME ANYTHING ABOUT THE VALUE OF THE LOOPING VARIABLE: IT MIGHT BE 8 ABOVE (THIS IS EXPLAINED OVERLEAF) *BUT IT MIGHT NOT.* BASICS *DIFFER.*

LOOPS (CONTINUED)

YOU SHOULD NEVER JUMP INTO THE MIDDLE OF A LOOP:

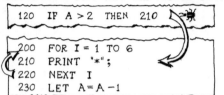

```
120   IF A > 2  THEN  210
```

```
200   FOR I = 1 TO 6
210   PRINT "*";
220   NEXT I
230   LET A = A - 1
```

BASIC WOULD NOT
OBEY A "NEXT"
IF IT HAD NOT
PREVIOUSLY OBEYED
THE MATCHING
"FOR".

BUT IN MOST *BASICS* YOU MAY JUMP OUT OF A LOOP AND THEN
BACK IN AGAIN (NOT A VERY GOOD PRACTICE).

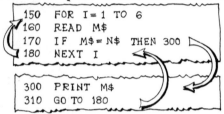

```
150   FOR I = 1 TO 6
160   READ M$
170   IF  M$ = N$  THEN 300
180   NEXT I
```

```
300   PRINT M$
310   GO TO 180
```

THE JARGON FOR THIS
IS A LOOP WITH
EXTENDED RANGE.

IN GENERAL YOU SHOULD ENTER A LOOP THROUGH ITS "FOR"
STATEMENT AND EITHER :

> • FALL THROUGH AT THE "NEXT", OR
> • JUMP OUT AND STAY OUT.

IF YOU NEED EXTENDED RANGE THEN ACHIEVE IT USING
THE "GO SUB" INSTRUCTION DESCRIBED ON PAGE 52.

IF A PROGRAM IS NOT SUPPOSED TO EXECUTE A LOOP *AT ALL*
UNDER CERTAIN CONDITIONS THEN IT IS SAFEST TO TEST FOR
THOSE CONDITIONS, AND, IF THEY APPLY, TO AVOID THE LOOP
ALTOGETHER.

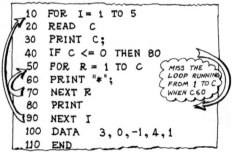

```
10    FOR I = 1 TO 5
20    READ C
30    PRINT C;
40    IF C <= 0 THEN 80
50    FOR R = 1 TO C
60    PRINT "*";
70    NEXT R
80    PRINT
90    NEXT I
100   DATA   3, 0, -1, 4, 1
110   END
```

MISS THE
LOOP RUNNING
FROM 1 TO C
WHEN C≤0

```
RUN

   3 ***
   0
  -1
   4 ****
   1 *
```

THE REASON FOR THIS
PRECAUTION IS GIVEN
OPPOSITE.

ALTHOUGH THE CONCEPT SEEMS SIMPLE THERE ARE HIDDEN DANGERS WITH LOOPS; DIFFERENT *BASICS* DEAL WITH THEM DIFFERENTLY. HERE IS THE INTERPRETATION IN MORE THAN ONE *STANDARD BASIC*.

CONSIDER THIS LOOP:

WHERE A, Z & S COULD BE COMPLICATED EXPRESSIONS ≈

```
10   FOR   V = A   TO Z   STEP S
         BODY
40   NEXT V
```

THE INTERPRETATION INVOLVES 3 VARIABLES WHICH *BASIC* ITSELF CAN USE BUT WHICH YOU, *THE USER*, CAN NEITHER REFER TO NOR CHANGE. CALL THEM:

♂   ♀   🐟
MARS   VENUS   &   FISH

START

LET V = A
LET ♂ = Z
LET ♀ = S

e.g. IN THE LOOP "FOR V = 1 TO 3" 🐟 BECOMES SUCCESSIVELY −2, −1, 0 THEN +1 ON EXIT

LET 🐟 = (V − ♂) * SGN(♀)

TEST 🐟   🐟 > 0

🐟 ≤ 0

"FALLS THROUGH" PAST NEXT V EVEN IF THE **BODY** HAS NEVER BEEN EXECUTED. *e.g.* FOR V = 1 TO 0 STEP +1 ♂ ♀

BUT SOME BASICS EXECUTE THE BODY AT LEAST ONCE REGARDLESS OF A, Z & S HENCE THE PRECAUTION OPPOSITE.

EXECUTE **BODY** DOWN TO "NEXT V"

LET V = V + ♀

V HAS A VALUE OF "THE NEXT VALUE NOT USED" BUT IN SOME BASICS IT WOULD BE **UNDEFINED** !

THIS LOGIC IMPLIES NO MATTER WHAT CHANGES YOU MAKE TO A, Z OR S IN THE BODY OF THE LOOP IT WILL NOT AFFECT THE NUMBER OF TIMES ROUND THE LOOP. BUT YOU SHOULD *NEVER* CHANGE THE VALUE OF V IN THE BODY OF THE LOOP.

REMEMBERING THAT MANY *BASICS* DON'T USE THIS LOGIC, *NEVER CHANGE ANYTHING IN THE BODY THAT COULD ALTER THE VALUE OF V, A, Z OR S. KEEP THE CONTROLS SIMPLE !*

GO SUB — RETURN

IN MANY PROGRAMS A PARTICULAR SEQUENCE OF INSTRUCTIONS OCCURS SEVERAL TIMES. IN SUCH CASES YOU DON'T HAVE TO *REPRODUCE* THAT SEQUENCE SEVERAL TIMES; YOU MAY PARCEL IT UP AS A *SUBROUTINE* AND SIMPLY <u>GO</u> TO THAT <u>SUB</u>ROUTINE FROM ANY LINE IN THE PROGRAM AND <u>RETURN</u> TO THE PLACE FROM WHENCE YOU CAME.

THE PROGRAM CALLED "OLD GLORY" ON PAGE 49 HAS A SEQUENCE OCCURRING THREE TIMES:

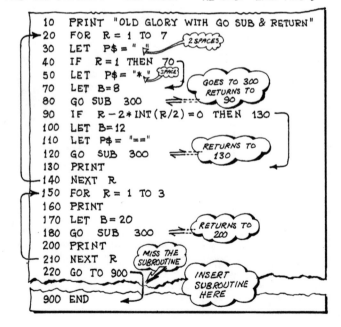

> FOR C = 1 TO *something*
> PRINT *something* ;
> NEXT C

WHICH COULD BE PARCELLED UP AS A SUBROUTINE:

```
300  REM  SUBROUTINE WITH B & P$
310  FOR  I = 1 TO B
320  PRINT  P$;
330  NEXT  I
340  RETURN
```

AND THE PROGRAM "OLD GLORY" RE-CAST LIKE THIS:

```
10    PRINT "OLD GLORY WITH GO SUB & RETURN"
20    FOR  R = 1 TO 7          2 SPACES
30    LET  P$ = " "
40    IF  R = 1 THEN  70
50    LET  P$ = "*"            SPACE
70    LET  B = 8
80    GO SUB 300               GOES TO 300
                               RETURNS TO 90
90    IF  R - 2*INT(R/2) = 0  THEN 130
100   LET  B = 12
110   LET  P$ = "=="
120   GO  SUB 300              RETURNS TO 130
130   PRINT
140   NEXT  R
150   FOR  R = 1 TO 3
160   PRINT
170   LET  B = 20
180   GO  SUB  300             RETURNS TO 200
200   PRINT
210   NEXT  R                  MISS THE SUBROUTINE
220   GO TO 900                INSERT SUBROUTINE HERE

900   END
```

THE FORM OF THE INSTRUCTION IS:

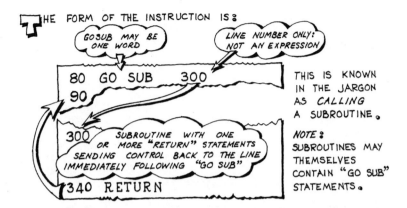

GOSUB MAY BE ONE WORD

LINE NUMBER ONLY: NOT AN EXPRESSION

80 GO SUB 300
90

THIS IS KNOWN IN THE JARGON AS *CALLING* A SUBROUTINE.

300 SUBROUTINE WITH ONE OR MORE "RETURN" STATEMENTS SENDING CONTROL BACK TO THE LINE IMMEDIATELY FOLLOWING "GO SUB"

340 RETURN

NOTE: SUBROUTINES MAY THEMSELVES CONTAIN "GO SUB" STATEMENTS.

"GO SUB" MAY BE ANYWHERE IN THE PROGRAM; THE SUBROUTINE BEING CALLED MAY ALSO BE ANYWHERE (NOT NECESSARILY ON HIGHER-NUMBERED LINES). YOU NEED CAREFUL ORGANIZATION TO PREVENT AN IMPOSSIBLE TANGLE.

A FEW *BASICS* ALLOW *DUMMY PARAMETERS* IN A SUBROUTINE. (THEY WORK IN THE MANNER EXPLAINED ON PAGE 26 IN CONNECTION WITH DUMMY ARGUMENTS OF FUNCTIONS.) HERE AGAIN DETAILS VARY A LOT FROM *BASIC* TO *BASIC* AND YOU SHOULDN'T USE DUMMY PARAMETERS IF YOU WANT "PORTABLE" PROGRAMS.

TAKE CARE NOT TO "FALL" INTO A SUBROUTINE BY ACCIDENT. NOTICE LINE 220 OPPOSITE: IF THIS WERE OMITTED THERE WOULD BE SUCH A "FALL".

CONTINUED OVERLEAF.

GO SUB (CONTINUED)

NOVICES TO PROGRAMMING MAY CARE TO SKIP THIS DOUBLE PAGE THE FIRST TIME THROUGH THE BOOK

"GO SUB" MAY APPEAR ANYWHERE IN A PROGRAM; LIKEWISE THE SUBROUTINE BEING CALLED MAY BE ANYWHERE. BASIC HAS NO SURE WAY OF ASSOCIATING A "RETURN" WITH THE PARTICULAR "GO SUB" OF *YOUR* INTENTION. (IT'S NOT LIKE "FOR V =" FOLLOWED BY "NEXT V" WHERE THE "V" MAKES THE ASSOCIATION CLEAR.) SO WE DESCRIBE BELOW HOW BASIC IS ABLE TO MAKE SUCH AN ASSOCIATION.

SOME BASICS DEAL WITH "GO SUB" BY A TECHNIQUE CALLED *STACKING.* THE STACK WORKS LIKE THIS:

WHEN BASIC MEETS "GO SUB" IT NOTES THE NUMBER OF THE LINE IMMEDIATELY FOLLOWING "GO SUB" AND PUTS THIS NUMBER ON THE TOP OF THE STACK; THEN CONTROL GOES TO THE LINE NOMINATED AFTER "GO SUB".

WHEN BASIC MEETS A "RETURN" IT SIMPLY LOOKS AT THE NUMBER CURRENTLY AT THE *TOP* OF THE STACK; GOES STRAIGHT TO THE LINE HAVING THAT NUMBER; THEN *THROWS AWAY* THAT NUMBER FROM THE TOP OF THE STACK.

THIS LOGIC IMPLIES THAT IF BASIC MEETS A "RETURN" BEFORE THE VERY FIRST "GO SUB" THEN THERE WILL BE AN EMPTY STACK, HENCE NOWHERE TO GO — OFTEN A BUG IN THE PROGRAM CAUSING CONTROL TO "FALL" INTO A SUBROUTINE. ON THE OTHER HAND BASIC MAY KEEP MEETING "GO SUB" BUT NOT ENOUGH "RETURNS" RESULTING IN THE STACK FILLING TO CAPACITY (WHICH VARIES FROM BASIC TO BASIC BUT IS TYPICALLY 10).

ALTHOUGH NOT ALL BASICS USE THIS PRECISE MECHANISM FOR HANDLING "GO SUB" YOU MAY *THINK* OF IT THIS WAY WHEN TESTING THE PROPOSED LOGIC OF A PROGRAM YOU ARE GOING TO WRITE, WHEN TRACKING DOWN BUGS IN A PROGRAM, AND WHEN TRYING TO FIGURE OUT THE LOGIC OF SOMEONE ELSE'S PROGRAM.

WHETHER OR NOT YOUR OWN BASIC HANDLES "GO SUB" USING A STACK IS ONLY IMPORTANT IF YOU WRITE A SUBROUTINE THAT *CALLS ITSELF.* THIS IS KNOWN AS *RECURSION* AND IS ONLY FEASIBLE WITH THE LOGIC OF THE STACK EXPLAINED ABOVE.

THIS STACK SHOWS THAT THE LAST "GO SUB" TO BE OBEYED IS THE SAME AS THE PREVIOUS ONE ⟲ INDICATING THAT A SUBROUTINE HAS JUST CALLED ITSELF *DIRECTLY*. EARLIER A SUBROUTINE HAD CALLED ANOTHER WHICH, IN TURN, HAD CALLED THE FIRST ONE. AS SHOWN BY THE ✭ ON THE PICTURE. THUS A SUBROUTINE HAD CALLED ITSELF *INDIRECTLY*.

YOU MAY DISCOVER IF YOUR VERSION OF *BASIC* ALLOWS SUBROUTINES TO CALL THEMSELVES. TRY THE FOLLOWING LITTLE PROGRAM WHICH FINDS THE HIGHEST COMMON FACTOR OF TWO NUMBERS BY EUCLID'S METHOD.

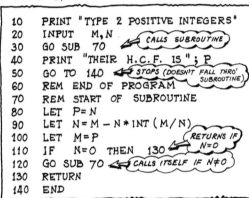

```
10    PRINT "TYPE 2 POSITIVE INTEGERS"
20    INPUT  M, N          ← CALLS SUBROUTINE
30    GO SUB  70
40    PRINT "THEIR H.C.F. IS "; P
50    GO TO 140            ← STOPS (DOESN'T FALL THRO' SUBROUTINE)
60    REM END OF PROGRAM
70    REM START OF SUBROUTINE
80    LET  P = N
90    LET  N = M - N * INT (M / N)
100   LET  M = P           RETURNS IF N=0
110   IF   N = 0  THEN  130
120   GO SUB 70            ← CALLS ITSELF IF N≠0
130   RETURN
140   END
```

YOUR OWN *BASIC* MAY WELL SAY THERE ARE NOT ENOUGH "RETURNS" ⟲ IN WHICH CASE IT PROBABLY DOESN'T USE THE LOGIC OF A STACK. ⟨ YOU MAY THEN CHANGE LINE 120 TO "GO TO 70" AND IT SHOULD WORK. ⟩

IF YOUR *BASIC* ACCEPTS THE PROGRAM WITHOUT ANY ALTERATION TO LINE 120 THEN YOU MAY EXPERIMENT TO FIND THE LIMITING HEIGHT OF THE STACK. THUS IF YOU TYPE 85, 204 THE PROGRAM WILL PRINT THE RESULT WHICH IS 17. BUT IF YOU TYPE 85, 289 THEN THE ALLOWABLE STACKING HEIGHT WILL PROBABLY BE EXCEEDED ALTHOUGH THE ANSWER IS STILL 17.

TRY " PLAYING COMPUTERS" USING PENCIL, PAPER AND POCKET CALCULATOR. THIS SHOULD REVEAL EUCLID'S METHOD AND ALSO SHOW HOW THE STACK BUILDS UP AND COLLAPSES.

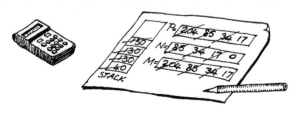

 THIS IS AN INFURIATING GAME.

THE PROGRAM SHOWN HERE WAS DESIGNED TO PLAY "MOO" AND ILLUSTRATE "GO SUB".

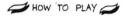 HOW TO PLAY

 START BY THROWING TWO DICE. AS EACH DIE IS CAST TYPE ITS SCORE ON THE KEYBOARD. (THIS MAKES SURE YOU DON'T PLAY THE SAME GAME EVERY TIME.)

 THE COMPUTER CHOOSES A NUMBER WITH FOUR DIGITS *NO TWO ALIKE* (NOTE: THE FIRST DIGIT COULD BE ZERO) .

 YOU GUESS WHAT NUMBER THE COMPUTER HAS CHOSEN AND TYPE YOUR GUESS WHEN INVITED TO DO SO.

THE COMPUTER NOTES HOW MANY OF YOUR DIGITS ARE RIGHT *BUT IN THE WRONG PLACE* EACH OF THESE IT CALLS A *COW*.

 THE COMPUTER NOTES HOW MANY OF YOUR DIGITS ARE NOT ONLY RIGHT *BUT ALSO IN THE RIGHT PLACE* EACH OF THESE IT CALLS A *BULL*.

HAVING REPORTED YOUR SCORE OF *BULLS & COWS* THE COMPUTER INVITES YOU TO GUESS AGAIN AND SO ON UNTIL YOU SCORE *FOUR* BULLS AND *NO* COWS.

HERE IS THE PROGRAM:

```
 5    REM     THE GAME OF MOO
10    PRINT  "THROW TWO DICE"
15    INPUT  I, J
20    FOR  K = 0  TO  6*I +J -7
25    LET  X = RND          POSSIBLY RND(0)
30    NEXT  K
35    REM    NOW FOR THE PROGRAM PROPER
```

```
110   LET X=INT(10000*RND)
120   LET Y= X
130   GO SUB 1000
140   IF C > O THEN 110
150   REM   NO COWS ON COMPARISON WITH SELF
160   PRINT "I HAVE CHOSEN A 4-DIGIT NUMBER"
170   LET T=0
180   LET T=T+1
190   PRINT "WHAT'S YOUR GUESS"
200   INPUT X
210   GO SUB 1000
220   PRINT B; "BULLS &"; C; "COWS"
230   IF B < 4 THEN 180
240   PRINT "THAT TOOK";T; "TRIES"
250   PRINT
260   GO TO 110
265   REM   STOP THIS GAME WITH 'BREAK' KEY
1000  REM          SUBROUTINE
1010  LET  B=0
1020  LET  C=0
1030  FOR  I = 1 TO 4
1040  LET  K = 10↑I
1050  LET  L = INT(10*(X-K*INT(X/K)+.1)/K)
1060  FOR  J = 1 TO 4
1070  LET  M= 10↑J
1075  LET  P = INT(10*(Y-M*INT(Y/M)+.1)/M)
1080  IF  L <> P THEN 1130
1090  LET  C= C+1
1100  IF  I <> J THEN 1130
1110  LET  C = C-1
1120  LET  B = B+1
1130  NEXT J
1140  NEXT I
1150  RETURN
1160  REM
1200  END

RUN

THROW 2 DICE
? 6,3
I HAVE CHOSEN A 4-DIGIT NUMBER
WHAT'S YOUR GUESS
? 1234
 O BULLS & 2 COWS
WHAT'S  YOUR  GUESS
? 5678
THAT TOOK 6 TRIES
```

Annotations:
- CHECK NO TWO DIGITS ALIKE
- COUNT THE TRIES
- COMPARE GUESS WITH NUMBER
- START A NEW GAME
- BULLS
- COWS
- PICK EACH DIGIT OF GUESS IN TURN
- COMPARE EACH DIGIT OF NUMBER WITH I th DIGIT OF GUESS
- THE 0·1 COMPENSATES FOR ROUNDING ERRORS, INT(3.99999) IS 3, INT(3.99999 + ·1) IS 4
- AND SO ON
- EVENTUALLY

57

ARRAYS

 IN *ADDITION* TO THE *SIMPLE*
NUMERICAL & TEXTUAL VARIABLES
YOU MAY USE THOUSANDS OF OTHER
VARIABLES ARRANGED IN *ARRAYS*.

BELOW IS AN EXAMPLE OF A *ONE-DIMENSIONAL* NUMERICAL ARRAY
CALLED A( ).

A(1)	3.56
A(2)	7.12
A(3)	10.68
A(4)	

A( ) HAS *ELEMENTS*, EACH OF WHICH CAN STORE
A NUMBER IN THE SAME WAY AS ANY *SIMPLE*
NUMERICAL VARIABLE :

```
100   LET   A(1) = 3.56
110   LET   A(2) = 7.12
120   LET   A(3) = A(1) + A(2)
```

ANOTHER NAME FOR *ELEMENT* IS *SINGLY-SUBSCRIPTED VARIABLE*
(OR JUST *SUBSCRIPTED VARIABLE* IF THE CONTEXT ALLOWS).

OTHER NAMES FOR A ONE-DIMENSIONAL ARRAY ARE : *VECTOR*,
COLUMN VECTOR, & *COLUMN MATRIX*. YOU CAN ALSO THINK OF
A( ) AS A ROW :

	A(1)	A(2)	A(3)	A(4)
	3.56	7.12	10.68	

AND CALL IT A *ROW VECTOR* OR *ROW MATRIX*.

BELOW IS AN EXAMPLE OF A *TWO-DIMENSIONAL* NUMERICAL
ARRAY CALLED B(,). IT HAS 4 ROWS AND 3 COLUMNS.

	1)	2)	3)
B(1,	8.92		
B(2,		17.84	-8.92
B(3,			
B(4,			

JUST AS WITH A( ), B(,) HAS
ELEMENTS EACH OF WHICH CAN
STORE A NUMBER IN THE SAME
WAY AS A SIMPLE NUMERICAL
VARIABLE :

```
130   LET   B(1,1) = 8.92
140   LET   B(2,2) = 2 * B(1,1)
150   LET   B(2,3) = -B(1,1)
```

ANOTHER NAME FOR AN ELEMENT OF A *TWO*-DIMENSIONAL ARRAY
IS *DOUBLY-SUBSCRIPTED VARIABLE* (OR JUST *SUBSCRIPTED
VARIABLE* WHEN THE CONTEXT ALLOWS).

OTHER NAMES FOR A TWO-DIMENSIONAL ARRAY ARE *RECTANGULAR
ARRAY* AND *RECTANGULAR MATRIX*. (IF THE NUMBER OF ROWS
IS THE SAME AS THE NUMBER OF COLUMNS THEN *SQUARE*
MAY BE SAID IN PLACE OF *RECTANGULAR*.)

A FEW *BASICS* ALLOW *THREE*-DIMENSIONAL ARRAYS.

BELOW IS AN EXAMPLE OF A *TEXTUAL* ARRAY CALLED T$(). IT IS *ONE-DIMENSIONAL* (SEVERAL *BASICS* DON'T ALLOW TWO-DIMENSIONAL TEXTUAL ARRAYS SO FOR THE SAKE OF "PORTABILITY" IT IS BEST TO DO WITHOUT THEM).

T$(1)	HO
T$(2)	
T$(3)	KEGRAPHA
T$(4)	
T$(5)	KEGRAPHA

T$( ) HAS ELEMENTS EACH OF WHICH CAN STORE A TEXT IN THE SAME WAY (AND USUALLY TO THE SAME LENGTH) AS ANY SIMPLE TEXTUAL VARIABLE.

```
160   LET   T$(1) = "HO"
170   LET   T$(3) = "KEGRAPHA"
180   LET   T$(5) = T$(3)
```

YOUR PROGRAM MAY HAVE UP TO 26 NUMERICAL ARRAYS:

$$A(\ ), \quad B(\ ), \quad C(\ ), \ldots, Z(\ )$$

OF WHICH SOME MAY BE *ONE*-DIMENSIONAL AND SOME *TWO*-DIMENSIONAL: ONE LETTER CAN'T BE MADE TO SERVE FOR BOTH KINDS AT ONCE.

YOUR PROGRAM MAY ALSO HAVE UP TO 26 TEXTUAL ARRAYS:

$$A\$(\ ), \quad B\$(\ ), \quad C\$(\ ), \ldots, Z\$(\ )$$

AND YOUR PROGRAM MAY USE ALL 286 SIMPLE NUMERICAL VARIABLES AND ALL 26 SIMPLE TEXTUAL VARIABLES WHICH ARE COMPLETELY DISTINCT FROM ELEMENTS OF ARRAYS: B(2,2) HAS NOTHING TO DO WITH B ; T$(5) HAS NOTHING TO DO WITH T$.

SPECIFY THE SIZES AND SHAPES OF THE ARRAYS YOU WANT TO USE BY THE "DIM" STATEMENT (SHORT FOR *DIMENSION*) AS EXPLAINED OVERLEAF. THE ARRAYS ON THIS DOUBLE PAGE WOULD BE SPECIFIED LIKE THIS:

```
10   REM   A PROGRAM WITH ARRAYS
20   DIM  A(4), B(4,3), T$(5)
```

61

 DIM IS SHORT FOR *DIMENSION*
USE THIS STATEMENT TO SPECIFY THE
DIMENSIONS OF *ALL* ARRAYS IN YOUR PROGRAM.

THE FOLLOWING SELECTION OF ARRAYS :

A$(1)
A$(2)
A$(3)
A$(4)

A(1)

C(1)   C(2)

	1)	2)	3)
B(1,			
B(2,			
B(3,			

MAY BE SPECIFIED IN ONE "DIM" STATEMENT :

```
10   REM    PROGRAM WITH ONE DIM
20   DIM    A$(4), A(1), C(2), B(3,3)
```

OR IN MORE THAN ONE "DIM" STATEMENT :

```
10   REM    PROGRAM WITH SEVERAL DIMS
20   DIM    C(2), A(1)     INTEGERS ONLY:
30   DIM    B(3,3)         EXPRESSIONS
40   DIM    A$(4)          NOT ALLOWED
```

MANY *BASICS* ALLOW YOU TO *OMIT* "DIM" STATEMENTS WHEN
DIMENSIONS ARE 10 OR LESS , BUT DON'T TAKE ADVANTAGE
OF THIS . IF YOU GO BACK TO A PROGRAM WRITTEN LONG
AGO ⌒ OR HAVE TO SORT OUT SOMEONE ELSE'S PROGRAM ⌒
IT IS HELPFUL TO KNOW STRAIGHT AWAY WHAT ARRAYS ARE
BEING USED . IN ANY CASE THERE ARE SOME *BASICS* THAT
DEMAND DECLARATION OF ALL ARRAYS HOWEVER SMALL .

ALL "DIM" STATEMENTS SHOULD BE NEAR THE BEGINNING
OF THE PROGRAM ⌒ BEFORE THE FIRST USE OF ANY
SUBSCRIPTED VARIABLES AFFECTED ⌒ AND YOU SHOULD ENSURE
THAT "DIM" STATEMENTS (LIKE "DEF" STATEMENTS ON
PAGE 26) ARE ACTUALLY ENCOUNTERED DURING EXECUTION.

```
50   LET   P(1) = 4·5
60   DIM   P(16)
```

```
10   GO TO 30
20   DIM A(40,40), B(1000)
30
```

IN MANY *BASICS* THESE THINGS DON'T MATTER BUT IN SOME
THEY *DO* ⌒ SO FOR THE SAKE OF "PORTABILITY" ACCEPT SUCH
LITTLE RESTRICTIONS.

IT IS ALWAYS A MISTAKE TO DECLARE
AN ARRAY MORE THAN ONCE .

```
10   DIM A(100,20), B(60)
20   DIM  B(60), C(500)
```

HISTORICALLY THE ROWS & COLUMNS OF ARRAYS IN *BASIC* WERE COUNTED FROM *ZERO* RATHER THAN UNITY.

	0)	1)	2)	3)
P(0,				
P(1,				
P(2,				

Q(0)	
Q(1)	
Q(2)	

AND THE "DIM" STATEMENT REFERRED TO *BIGGEST SUBSCRIPTS* RATHER THAN QUANTITIES OF ROWS AND COLUMNS:

```
10   REM    HISTORICAL BASIC
20   DIM    P(2,3) , Q(2)
```

BUT THERE ARE VERSIONS OF *BASIC* TODAY THAT COUNT FROM *UNITY* (AS IN THE ILLUSTRATIONS OPPOSITE) SO IT IS SAFEST TO *IMAGINE* YOUR VERSION COUNTS FROM 1. IF, IN FACT, IT COUNTS FROM ZERO IT MEANS YOU ARE WASTING SOME SPACE IN THE COMPUTER'S STORE BUT AT LEAST YOUR PROGRAM SHOULD BE "PORTABLE".

SOME *BASICS* CATER FOR BOTH METHODS WITH THE STATEMENT:

OR:
```
10   BASE   0
```
```
10   BASE   1
```

TO DECLARE WHETHER YOU WISH TO COUNT FROM ZERO OR UNITY RESPECTIVELY.

THE "DIM" STATEMENT MAKES *BASIC* RESERVE SPACE IN THE COMPUTER'S STORE FOR ALL YOUR ARRAYS, BUT THIS DOESN'T IMPLY THAT *BASIC* CLEARS THEM OF INFORMATION LEFT OVER FROM A PREVIOUS COMPUTER RUN. SOME *BASICS* DO SET SUBSCRIPTED VARIABLES TO ZERO (BLANKS IN THE CASE OF TEXTS), OTHERS "FLAG" THEM AS UNSET (AS DISCUSSED FOR SIMPLE VARIABLES ON PAGE 11), AND OTHERS LEAVE THEM FULL OF "GARBAGE". SO IF YOUR PROGRAM READS FROM AN ARRAY:

```
100   LET A = B(2,2)
```

EXPECTING TO FIND ZERO WHEN NOTHING HAS YET BEEN PUT THERE, *MAKE SURE YOUR PROGRAM CLEARS THE ARRAY FIRST.* THE SIMPLEST WAY TO DO THIS IS EXPLAINED ON PAGE 86 WHICH WE ANTICIPATE WITH THIS EXAMPLE:

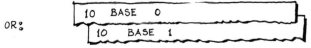

```
70   MAT  B = ZER
```

SETS ALL ELEMENTS OF ARRAY B(,) TO ZERO

SUBSCRIPTS

THE FOLLOWING ARRAY:

```
10 DIM  B(4,3)
```

	1)	2)	3)
B(1,			
B(2,			
B(3,			
B(4,			

IS AN ARRAY OF 12 SUBSCRIPTED VARIABLES EACH OF WHICH CAN BE USED AS THOUGH IT WERE A *SIMPLE* NUMERICAL VARIABLE:

```
100 LET  B(1,2) = B(2,2)↑2 + 6.8
110 LET  B(3,3) = FNC( B(1,1)/B(2,2))
120 PRINT  B(1,2); B(3,3)
130 FOR I = B(1,1) TO B(1,2) STEP B(1,3)
140 IF  B(3,3) >= B(2,3) THEN 600
```

EXAMPLES OF SYNTAX: THE CONTENT IS MEANINGLESS

THIS APPLIES TO TEXTUAL VARIABLES TOO:

```
150 LET  T$(6) = "PONZIO"
160 IF  T$(7) <> "PILATO" THEN 200
170 PRINT  T$(6); T$(7)
```

IN ANY EXPRESSION WHERE A *SIMPLE* VARIABLE IS ALLOWED A *SUBSCRIPTED* VARIABLE IS ALSO ALLOWED.

BUT THERE ARE PLACES OUTSIDE EXPRESSIONS WHERE YOU *CAN'T* HAVE A SUBSCRIPTED VARIABLE:

NOT AS A LOOPING VARIABLE:

```
180 FOR  B(1,1) = 1 TO 3
```

```
190 DEF FNC( B(1,1) ) = SQR(A↑2 + B↑2)
```

NOT AS THE DUMMY ARGUMENT OF A FUNCTION.

THE *REAL* ADVANTAGE OF SUBSCRIPTED VARIABLES, HOWEVER, IS NOT AS A SUBSTITUTE FOR SIMPLE VARIABLES BUT BECAUSE THEIR

SUBSCRIPTS MAY BE VARIABLES + EXPRESSIONS

EVEN COMPLICATED EXPRESSIONS, THEMSELVES CONTAINING SUBSCRIPTED VARIABLES.

THUS IT IS SIMPLE TO READ A ROW OR COLUMN VECTOR: ➡

```
200 DATA "A","B","C","D"
210 FOR I = 1 TO 4
220 READ T$(I)
230 NEXT I
```

```
240 FOR R = 1 TO 4
250 FOR C = 1 TO 3
260 LET B(R,C) = 0
270 NEXT C
280 NEXT R
```

◁ OR CLEAR A RECTANGULAR ARRAY ?

OR PRINT A VECTOR
(IN THIS CASE AS A ROW) ? ➡

```
290 FOR I = 1 TO 4
300 PRINT   T$(I);
310 NEXT I
320 PRINT
```

```
330 FOR  R = 1 TO 4
340 FOR  C = 1 TO 4
350 PRINT B(R,C);
360 NEXT C
370 PRINT
380 NEXT R
```

◁ OR PRINT A RECTANGULAR ARRAY
(IN THIS CASE BY ROWS) ?

OR SCAN A LIST OF ITEMS TO FIND THE LOCATION OF A PARTICULAR ITEM.

```
390 FOR  I = 1 TO 4
400 IF T$(I) =  "C" THEN 430
410 NEXT I
420 LET  I = 0
430 PRINT "LOCATION IS"; I
```

BUT **BEWARE** OF USING COMPLICATED EXPRESSIONS AS SUBSCRIPTS: ➡

```
440 LET X = B(A↑2/2 , 3)
```

WHAT WOULD HAPPEN IF A↑2/2 TURNED OUT TO BE 3.99999 ?

☆ SOME *BASICS* WOULD TAKE THE *INTEGRAL PART* OF THE RESULT AND LET X = B(3,3)

☆ OTHER *BASICS* WOULD TAKE THE *NEAREST INTEGER* TO THE RESULT AND LET X = B(4,3)

YOU CAN EASILY TEST WHAT YOUR OWN VERSION OF *BASIC* DOES BY RUNNING THE LITTLE PROGRAM BELOW. BUT YOU SHOULD NOT

```
10   DIM    A(2)
20   LET    A(1) = 100
30   LET    A(2) = 200
40   LET    I = 1.99
50   PRINT  A(I)
60   END
```

WRITE PROGRAMS THAT RELY ON ONE PARTICULAR INTERPRETATION. KEEP SUBSCRIPTS SIMPLE AND USE "INT( )" IF THEIR VALUES COULD HAVE FRACTIONAL PARTS.

SORTING NUMBERS INTO ASCENDING ORDER IS SIMPLE IN CONCEPT BUT SURPRISINGLY DIFFICULT TO ORGANISE WHEN THERE ARE LARGE VOLUMES OF DATA. THE EXAMPLE BELOW USES THE SIMPLEST TECHNIQUE OF ALL ➾ THE *RIPPLE* SORT ➾ WHICH IS ADEQUATE FOR SMALL VOLUMES OF DATA (100 OR SO NUMBERS) STORED AS ARRAYS IN *BASIC*.

A(1)	6.5
A(2)	13.9
A(3)	4.6
A(4)	10.2
A(5)	3.5

ARRAY A( ), A COLUMN VECTOR, IS TO BE SORTED INTO ASCENDING ORDER ➾ HEAVIEST NUMBERS SINKING TO THE BOTTOM. YOU CAN REVERSE THIS ORDER BY REVERSING THE CONDITION IN THE " IF " STATEMENT.

WE START WITH AN "INDEX" I POINTING TO ROW 1; THEN WE ADVANCE I ROW BY ROW. AT EVERY ADVANCE WE LOOK AT THE NUMBER I IS POINTING TO ➾ AND ALSO AT THE NUMBER ONE ROW AHEAD OF I. IF THE FORMER IS GREATER THAN THE LATTER WE SWOP THE TWO NUMBERS.

HAVING FINISHED ONE "SWEEP" OF I WE SWEEP AGAIN ➾ BUT STOP ONE ROW SHORT OF THE PREVIOUS SWEEP BECAUSE THE HEAVIEST NUMBER MUST ALREADY HAVE SUNK TO THE BOTTOM.

WE CONTINUE SWEEPING ➾ EACH SWEEP A ROW SHORTER THAN THE PREVIOUS ONE ➾ UNTIL THERE IS A WHOLE SWEEP WITHOUT A SINGLE SWOP IN IT OR THE LENGTH OF SWEEP IS REDUCED TO NOTHING.

HERE IS THE WHOLE PROCESS :)} SHOWS WHERE A SWOP HAS JUST OCCURRED :

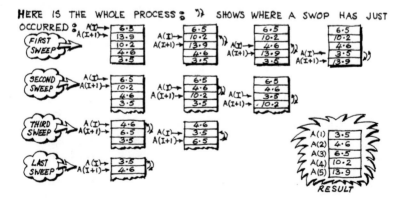

THE PROGRAM BELOW IS DESIGNED TO SORT A COLUMN VECTOR, A(),
HAVING N ROWS. THE VECTOR IS FILLED FROM "DATA" STATEMENTS
⬿ THE FIRST NUMBER IN THE FIRST "DATA" STATEMENT TELLING THE
NUMBER OF NUMBERS TO BE SORTED. THE LOGIC ILLUSTRATED HERE
IS USED AGAIN IN A MORE USEFUL WAY ON PAGE 71 WHERE WE
AVOID ACTUALLY HAVING TO MOVE THE NUMBERS BEING SORTED.

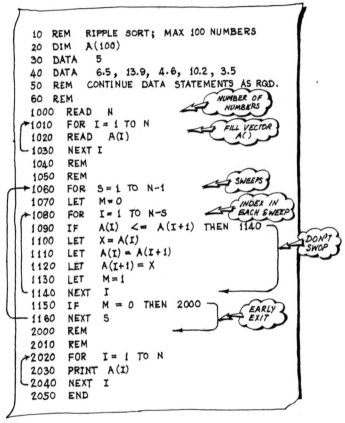

```
10    REM    RIPPLE SORT; MAX 100 NUMBERS
20    DIM    A(100)
30    DATA   5
40    DATA   6.5, 13.9, 4.6, 10.2, 3.5
50    REM    CONTINUE DATA STATEMENTS AS RQD.
60    REM                              NUMBER OF
1000  READ   N                         NUMBERS
1010  FOR    I = 1 TO N                 FILL VECTOR
1020  READ   A(I)                       A( )
1030  NEXT   I
1040  REM
1050  REM                              SWEEPS
1060  FOR    S = 1 TO N-1
1070  LET    M = 0                     INDEX IN
1080  FOR    I = 1 TO N-S              EACH SWEEP
1090  IF     A(I) <= A(I+1) THEN 1140
1100  LET    X = A(I)                       DON'T
1110  LET    A(I) = A(I+1)                  SWOP
1120  LET    A(I+1) = X
1130  LET    M = 1
1140  NEXT   I
1150  IF     M = 0 THEN 2000
1160  NEXT   S                         EARLY
2000  REM                              EXIT
2010  REM
2020  FOR    I = 1 TO N
2030  PRINT  A(I)
2040  NEXT   I
2050  END
```

VARIABLE M IS A "MARK" SET ZERO BEFORE EACH SWEEP BUT
SET NON-ZERO EVERY TIME THERE IS A SWOP. M IS
TESTED AT THE END OF EACH SWEEP AND IF IT SHOWS THERE
WERE NO SWOPS THEN CONTROL JUMPS TO AN EARLY EXIT.

THIS TECHNIQUE ⬿ AND OTHERS USED IN THE LONGER EXAMPLES IN
THIS BOOK ⬿ ARE EXPLAINED VERY CLEARLY BY A. COLIN DAY IN
"FORTRAN TECHNIQUES" ꞉ CAMBRIDGE UNIVERSITY PRESS (1972).

CHAINS ILLUSTRATE THE USEFULNESS OF SUBSCRIPTS. THE MANIPULATION OF CHAINS IS CALLED *LIST PROCESSING*.

THE SIMPLEST KIND OF CHAIN IS ILLUSTRATED BELOW. IT HAS A *HEAD* IN THE FORM OF A SIMPLE VARIABLE, H. THIS STORES A *POINTER* POINTING TO THE FIRST ROW OF INFORMATION SOMEWHERE IN ARRAY A(,) ⟺ POINTING ALSO TO A *LINK* CONTAINING ANOTHER POINTER POINTING TO THE *NEXT* ROW OF INFORMATION IN A(,). THE LAST LINK IN THE CHAIN CONTAINS A *ZERO* SAYING " END OF CHAIN ".

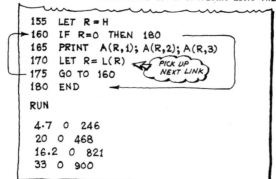

	1)	2)	3)
A(1,	6.3	−1	123
A(2,	4.7	0	246
A(3,	20.0	0	468
A(4,	16.2	0	821
A(5,	19.0	−1	333
A(6,	33.0	0	900

THE FOLLOWING PIECE OF PROGRAM WOULD PRINT INFORMATION IN A(,) ORGANISED BY THE CHAIN WITH HEAD H ⟺ HOWEVER LONG THE CHAIN.

```
155  LET R = H
160  IF R=0 THEN 180
165  PRINT  A(R,1); A(R,2); A(R,3)
170  LET R= L(R)        PICK UP
                        NEXT LINK
175  GO TO 160
180  END

RUN

4.7  0  246
20   0  468
16.2 0  821
33   0  900
```

THE CLEAREST WAY TO DRAW A CHAIN IS TO HOLD THE HEAD IN ONE HAND, THE LAST LINK IN THE OTHER, AND PULL TIGHT. THE CHAIN ILLUSTRATED ABOVE NOW LOOKS LIKE THIS:

H [2] → L(2) [3] → L(3) [4] → L(4) [6] → L(6) [0]

WE USE THIS MODEL TO EXPLAIN SOME OPERATIONS ON CHAINS.

A NEW ROW OF A(,) MAY BE LINKED INTO THE CHAIN LIKE THIS:

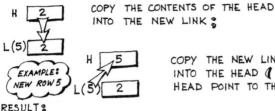

COPY THE CONTENTS OF THE HEAD INTO THE NEW LINK;

EXAMPLE: NEW ROW 5

COPY THE NEW LINK'S SUBSCRIPT INTO THE HEAD (THUS MAKING THE HEAD POINT TO THE NEW LINK).

RESULT:

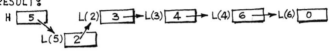

THE FOLLOWING SUBROUTINE LINKS ROW N INTO A CHAIN STORED IN VECTOR L( ) AND HEAD IN VARIABLE H:

```
100    REM LINK ROW N TO CHAIN L( ) HEAD H
110    LET L(N) = H
120    LET H = N
130    RETURN
```

SO LINKING ROW 5 TO THE CHAIN (PICTURED ABOVE) CAN BE DONE VERY SIMPLY LIKE THIS:

```
1055    LET N = 5
1060    GO SUB 100
1065
```

AND CREATING A NEW CHAIN TO LINK, SAY, THE FIRST 10 ROWS LIKE THIS:

```
2125    LET H = 0        BEGIN WITH EMPTY CHAIN
2130    FOR N = 1 TO 10
2135    GO SUB 100
2140    NEXT N
```

NOTICE THE *LAST* ROW TO BE LINKED TO A CHAIN IN THIS WAY IS THE *FIRST* TO BE PRINTED BY THE ROUTINE OPPOSITE. THUS THE MECHANISM MAY BE USED TO ORGANIZE A *STACK* OF THE KIND DESCRIBED ON PAGE 54. TAKING AN ELEMENT FROM THE TOP OF THE STACK MAY BE DONE LIKE THIS:

```
3260    LET R = H        REMEMBER THE ROW OF THE ELEMENT
3265    LET H = L(H)     DISCARD TOP LINK
```

CHAINS (CONTINUED)

IT MAKES FOR TIDIER PROGRAMS TO STORE HEADS OF CHAINS IN THE SAME VECTOR AS THE LINKS. THIS WASTES A FEW STORAGE LOCATIONS (AS SHOWN BELOW) BUT YOU MAY REGAIN THE SPACE BY OFFSETTING THE CHAIN FROM ITS INFORMATION AT THE EXPENSE OF MORE COMPLICATED SUBSCRIPTS IF YOU WISH.

MORE THAN ONE CHAIN CAN EXIST IN THE SAME VECTOR AS LONG AS THE ROWS BEING LINKED ARE MUTUALLY EXCLUSIVE (*i.e.* NO LINK CAN BE IN MORE THAN ONE CHAIN). THE SUBROUTINE BELOW LINKS WOMEN INTO ONE CHAIN AND MEN INTO ANOTHER. THE HEADS OF BOTH CHAINS ARE AT THE TOP OF THE VECTOR STORING BOTH CHAINS.

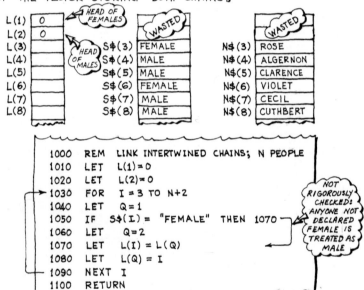

```
1000   REM   LINK INTERTWINED CHAINS; N PEOPLE
1010   LET   L(1) = 0
1020   LET   L(2) = 0
1030   FOR   I = 3 TO N+2
1040   LET   Q = 1
1050   IF    S$(I) = "FEMALE" THEN 1070
1060   LET   Q = 2
1070   LET   L(I) = L(Q)
1080   LET   L(Q) = I
1090   NEXT  I
1100   RETURN
```

NOT RIGOROUSLY CHECKED: ANYONE NOT DECLARED FEMALE IS TREATED AS MALE

IN THE SORTING PROGRAM ON PAGE 66 WE EXCHANGED ITEMS OF DATA. WITH CHAINED LISTS, HOWEVER, IT IS ONLY NECESSARY TO EXCHANGE *LINKS* WHEN SORTING. CONSIDER THIS SHORT LENGTH OF CHAIN:

→L(8) [7] →L(7) [3] →L(3) [5] →L(5) [

TO *EFFECTIVELY* SWOP ROWS 7 & 3 OF THE ARRAY ASSOCIATED WITH THIS CHAIN YOU NEED ONLY SHUNT THREE POINTERS AROUND THE LINKS AS ILLUSTRATED OPPOSITE.

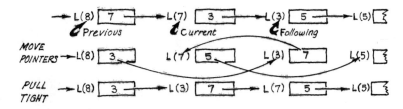

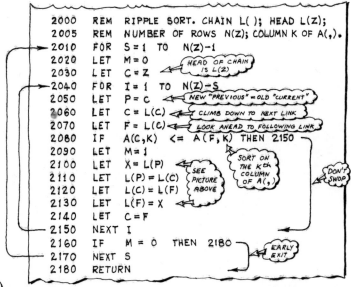

THE SUBROUTINE BELOW USES THE SAME LOGIC AS THE PROGRAM ON PAGE 67 ⟿ THE *RIPPLE* SORT ⟿ BUT WHENEVER IT HAS TO SWOP ROWS IT MOVES POINTERS IN THE MANNER ILLUSTRATED ABOVE. THE LOGIC FOR THIS IS ON LINES 2100 TO 2130 , WHERE :

> **P** IS A SUBSCRIPT FOR THE *PREVIOUS* LINK ,
> **C** IS A SUBSCRIPT FOR THE *CURRENT* LINK ,
> **F** IS A SUBSCRIPT FOR THE *FOLLOWING* LINK ,

ALL AS SHOWN IN THE PICTURE ABOVE. AFTER A SWOP , **C** IS NO LONGER THE CURRENT SUBSCRIPT ; IT IS ALTERED AT LINE 2140 .

```
2000   REM   RIPPLE SORT. CHAIN L( ); HEAD L(Z);
2005   REM   NUMBER OF ROWS N(Z); COLUMN K OF A(,).
2010   FOR   S = 1 TO N(Z)-1
2020   LET   M = 0
2030   LET   C = Z              HEAD OF CHAIN IS L(Z)
2040   FOR   I = 1 TO N(Z)-S
2050   LET   P = C              NEW "PREVIOUS" = OLD "CURRENT"
2060   LET   C = L(C)           CLIMB DOWN TO NEXT LINK
2070   LET   F = L(C)           LOOK AHEAD TO FOLLOWING LINK
2080   IF    A(C,K) <= A(F,K) THEN 2150
2090   LET   M = 1
2100   LET   X = L(P)           SEE PICTURE ABOVE / SORT ON THE Kth COLUMN OF A(,) / DON'T SWOP
2110   LET   L(P) = L(C)
2120   LET   L(C) = L(F)
2130   LET   L(F) = X
2140   LET   C = F
2150   NEXT  I
2160   IF    M = 0 THEN 2180    EARLY EXIT
2170   NEXT  S
2180   RETURN
```

◉THER DIFFERENCES FROM THE PROGRAM ON PAGE 67 ARE NOT CONCERNED WITH THE LOGIC OF SORTING. THE ROUTINE ABOVE CAN USE *ANY* CHAIN STORED IN L( ) BEING TOLD A VALUE OF Z : THE HEAD OF THE REQUIRED CHAIN IS THEN L(Z) AND THE NUMBER OF ITEMS IS IN N(Z). FURTHERMORE THE ROUTINE ABOVE CAN SORT *ANY* COLUMN OF ARRAY A(,) BEING TOLD THE NUMBER OF THAT COLUMN IN K.

 AN *EXAMPLE*
USING THE SIMPLE LIST
PROCESSING TECHNIQUES
JUST DESCRIBED.

THE TYPICAL "MANAGEMENT REPORTING" PROGRAM DEALS WITH "POPULATIONS BROKEN DOWN BY AGE, RELIGION AND SEX". THE FOLLOWING PROGRAM IS A GHASTLY PARODY OF THE REAL THING BUT SERVES TO ILLUSTRATE A FEW OF THE TECHNIQUES AT THE HEART OF BUSINESS DATA PROCESSING. THE PROGRAM SORTS DIFFERENT COLUMNS OF NUMBERS. IT IS LEFT AS AN EXERCISE FOR THE READER TO EXTEND THE PROGRAM TO SORT NAMES ALPHABETICALLY (SEE PAGE 41 ON THIS).

THIS PROGRAM CALLS THE TWO SUBROUTINES GIVEN ON THE PREVIOUS DOUBLE PAGE. TO USE THE PROGRAM YOU TYPE THE NAME, SEX, DEPARTMENT NUMBER, AGE & SALARY OF EACH MEMBER OF STAFF OF A DEPARTMENT STORE. THE PROGRAM THEN PRINTS THREE MANAGEMENT REPORTS EACH OF WHICH DEALS SEPARATELY WITH THE SEXES. THE FIRST REPORT TABULATES THE INPUT DATA ORDERED BY DEPARTMENT NUMBER, THE SECOND ORDERED BY AGE OF EMPLOYEE, THE THIRD BY SALARY. IN ALL THREE REPORTS THE "ORDERING" COLUMN IS KEPT NEXT TO THE COLUMN OF NAMES.

AN IMPORTANT THING TO NOTICE ABOUT THIS PROGRAM IS THAT THE ORIGINAL INPUT DATA ARE NEVER MOVED. ORGANIZATION IS BY SHUNTING POINTERS ABOUT IN A SINGLE LIST OF POINTERS.

```
10 PRINT "DEPARTMENT STORE:  STAFF ANALYSIS"
20 DIM N(2), L$(100), N$(100), M$(100), S$(100), A(100,3), T$(2), R$(3)
30 DATA "FEMALE", "MALE", "DEPARTMENT", "AGE", "SALARY"
40 READ T$(1),   T$(2), R$(1),       R$(2),   R$(3)
50 DEF   FNC(Y)=Y-3*INT(Y/4)
60 REM  FNC CYCLES 1,2,3,1,2 AS Y GOES 1 TO 5
70 PRINT "HOW MANY STAFF "        NUMBER OF STAFF
80 INPUT   N
90 PRINT "FIRSTNAME,LASTNAME,   SEX,   DEPT.,    AGE, SALARY"
100 LET  N(2)=0
110   FOR I = 3 TO N+2
120   INPUT   N$(I),   M$(I),  S$(I),  A(I,1),  A(I,2),  A(I,3)
130   IF   S$(I) = T$(1)  THEN  150
140   LET  N(2)=N(2)+1          COUNT THE
                                NUMBER OF
150   NEXT I                    MEN
160 LET N(1)= N - N(2)     NUMBER OF
170 REM   INPUT COMPLETE   WOMEN
```

```
180 REM    BEGIN ANALYSIS
190 GO SUB 1000
200 FOR K = 1 TO 3
210 PRINT
220 PRINT "REPORT"; K; "ORDERED BY "; R$(K)
230 PRINT
240   FOR Z = 1 TO 2
250   GO SUB 2000
260   PRINT
270   PRINT T$(Z); " STAFF"
280   PRINT "NAME" , , R$(K), R$( FNC(K+1) ), R$( FNC(K+2) )
290   LET R=L(Z)
300     IF R = 0 THEN 340
310     PRINT N$(R), M$(R), A(R,K), A(R, FNC(K+1)), A(R, FNC(K+2) )
320     LET R=L(R)
330     GO TO 300
340   NEXT Z
350 NEXT K
360 GO TO 9999
```

(annotations:)
- BEGIN ANALYSIS → CREATE TWO CHAINS; FEMALE & MALE
- → CYCLE 3 COLUMNS OF A(,) TO GIVE 3 REPORTS
- → SPACE
- FOR Z = 1 TO 2 → CYCLE WOMEN THEN MEN
- → SORT ON COLUMN K OF A(,)
- → SPACE
- → HEAD OF CHAIN
- → NEXT LINK
- 360 GO TO 9999 → DON'T FALL THROUGH SUBROUTINES

INSERT SUBROUTINES 1000 & 2000 HERE

```
9999 END

RUN

DEPARTMENT STORE:  STAFF ANALYSIS
HOW MANY STAFF
? 6
FIRSTNAME,LASTNAME,    SEX,    DEPT.,    AGE,  SALARY
? ROSE STAGG     FEMALE      6        21      2800
? ALGERNON SWEET   MALE     6        23      3750
? CLARENCE PETTY    MALE     7        22      3750
? VIOLET BUCK      FEMALE     6      66      2000
? CECIL WILTING    MALE      7      18      4000
? CUTHBERT MACQUEEN MALE      5      70      6000
```

THIS BECOMES THE FIRST COLUMN HEADING IN REPORT 2 — DITTO: REPORT 3

```
REPORT 1 ORDERED BY DEPARTMENT

FEMALE STAFF
NAME                    DEPARTMENT      AGE          SALARY
VIOLET      BUCK          6              66           2000
ROSE        STAGG         6              21           2800
MALE STAFF
 NAME                    DEPARTMENT      AGE          SALARY
CUTHBERT    MACQUEEN      5              70           6000
ALGERNON    SWEET         6              23           3750
CECIL       WILTING       7              18           4000
CLARENCE    PETTY         7              22           3750

REPORT 2 ORDERED BY AGE        etc. etc.
```

73

MATRICES

 **MATRICES†** ☞ *DON'T RUN AWAY* ☜ YOU DON'T HAVE TO KNOW MATRIX ALGEBRA TO FIND "MAT" STATEMENTS USEFUL.

IN *BASIC* A MATRIX IS SIMPLY A RECTANGULAR ARRAY OF SUBSCRIPTED VARIABLES :

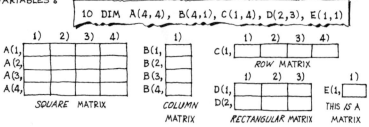

```
10 DIM A(4,4), B(4,1), C(1,4), D(2,3), E(1,1)
```

SQUARE MATRIX · COLUMN MATRIX · ROW MATRIX · RECTANGULAR MATRIX · THIS *IS* A MATRIX

AND THERE ARE ABOUT 12 **"MAT"** STATEMENTS IN MOST *BASICS* WITH WHICH YOU CAN *MANIPULATE* SUCH ARRAYS .

BUT WATCH OUT FOR THE FOLLOWING :

SOME *BASICS* ALLOW "MAT" STATEMENTS TO BE USED ON *ONE*-DIMENSIONAL ARRAYS BUT OTHERS DON'T. SO ALWAYS MAKE *TWO*-DIMENSIONAL ARRAYS WHEN YOU INTEND TO USE "MAT" STATEMENTS ☞ EVEN WHEN ONE OF THE DIMENSIONS IS UNITY (AS IN B(,), C(,) & E(,) ABOVE) .

DON'T OMIT "DIM" STATEMENTS FOR ARRAYS EVEN THOUGH MOST *BASICS* ALLOW SUCH OMISSION WHEN DIMENSIONS ARE 10 OR LESS (SEE PAGE 62) .

SOME *BASICS* ALLOW SUBSCRIPTS OF ZERO , BUT IN SPITE OF THIS THEIR "MAT" STATEMENTS **IGNORE** THE ZERO[th] ROW & ZERO[th] COLUMN (THUS SUPPORTING THE EXHORTATION ON PAGE 63 NEVER TO USE ZERO SUBSCRIPTS) . JUST IN CASE YOUR VERSION *DOES* ALLOW ZERO SUBSCRIPTS ☞ AND YOU CAN'T BE CERTAIN FROM ITS USER'S MANUAL WHETHER "MAT" STATEMENTS FOLLOW SUIT ☞ RUN THIS LITTLE PROGRAM. IF IT SHOULD PRINT 1 RATHER THAN 0 THEN PROBABLY ALL YOUR "MAT" STATEMENTS TAKE ACCOUNT OF THE ZERO[th] ROW & COLUMN ☞ AN UNUSUAL *BASIC* SYSTEM.

```
10 DIM A(1,1)
20 LET A(0,0)=0
30 MAT A = CON
40 PRINT A(0,0)
50 END
RUN      GOOD!
0
```

† matrix, *mā'triks* , or *mat'riks* , *n.* (math.) a rectangular array of quantities or symbols: *pl* ma'trices (*-tris-ēz*, or *iz*) [L *mātrix,icis,* a breeding animal, later, the womb – *mater*, mother]

ᴹᴬTRIX INSTRUCTIONS BEGIN WITH THE WORD "MAT". TWELVE OF THEM ARE LISTED BELOW AND DESCRIBED ON SUCCEEDING PAGES. TERMS LIKE "TRANSPOSITION", "MATRIX MULTIPLICATION", AND "INVERSION" ARE EXPLAINED SO THAT THOSE WHO HAVE NEVER MET MATRIX ALGEBRA MAY UNDERSTAND AND USE THE ASSOCIATED INSTRUCTIONS.

ᶠOR EVERY "MAT" INSTRUCTION THIS BOOK GIVES A CORRESPONDING ROUTINE IN ELEMENTARY *BASIC* USING NESTED LOOPS. IN ANY NEST OF LOOPS THE VARIABLE CONTROLLING THE INNERMOST LOOP VARIES FASTEST. IF *BASIC* STORES ARRAYS BY COLUMNS THEN IT IS MOST EFFICIENT TO MAKE THE *ROW* SUBSCRIPT VARY FASTEST & CONVERSELY IF *BASIC* STORES ARRAYS BY ROWS THEN IT IS BETTER TO MAKE THE *COLUMN* SUBSCRIPT VARY FASTEST. IT HAPPENS THAT SOME *BASICS* STORE ARRAYS BY COLUMNS ; OTHERS BY ROWS ; SO DON'T LOOK FOR SIGNIFICANCE IN THE CHOICE OF ROW & COLUMN SUBSCRIPTS IN THIS BOOK.

 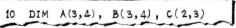

THIS INSTRUCTION MAKES A COPY OF A COMPLETE ARRAY.

```
10   DIM  A(3,4),  B(3,4),  C(2,3)
```

	1)	2)	3)	4)
A(1,				
A(2,				
A(3,				

	1)	2)	3)	4)
B(1,	5	-9.6	2.5	7.51
B(2,	6.3	0	1	2.34
B(3,	7.2	3.7	-1	8.86

	1)	2)	3)
C(1,	235	198	137
C(2,	642	856	705

Suppose YOU WANT ARRAY A(,) TO CONTAIN THE VALUES NOW CONTAINED IN ARRAY B(,). YOU CAN ACHIEVE THIS FAIRLY SIMPLY BY COPYING FROM B(,) TO A(,) ELEMENT BY ELEMENT LIKE THIS:

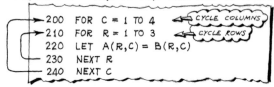

```
200   FOR C = 1 TO 4        CYCLE COLUMNS
210   FOR R = 1 TO 3        CYCLE ROWS
220   LET A(R,C) = B(R,C)
230   NEXT R
240   NEXT C
```

BUT YOU COULD DO THE WHOLE THING WITH A SINGLE "MAT" INSTRUCTION LIKE THIS:

```
100   MAT   A = B
```

NOTICE THAT A & B ON LINE 100 HAVE NOTHING WHATEVER TO DO WITH SIMPLE VARIABLES A & B. THE WORD "MAT" TELLS *BASIC* YOU MEAN *ARRAYS* A(,) & B(,).

With THE ARRAYS PICTURED ABOVE IT WOULD BE A MISTAKE TO HAVE LINE 110 AS SHOWN BELOW; B(,) IS TOO BIG TO FIT INSIDE C(,). BUT LINE 120 *IS* ALLOWED. IT HAS THE EFFECT OF *ALTERING* THE DIMENSIONS OF B(,) TO 2 ROWS AND 3 COLUMNS:

2 & 3 ARE NOW ITS **CURRENT DIMENSIONS**

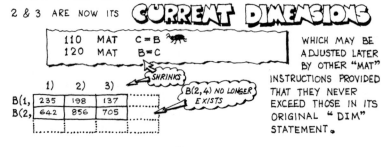

```
110   MAT   C = B
120   MAT   B = C
```

SHRINKS

B(2,4) NO LONGER EXISTS

	1)	2)	3)
B(1,	235	198	137
B(2,	642	856	705

WHICH MAY BE ADJUSTED LATER BY OTHER "MAT" INSTRUCTIONS PROVIDED THAT THEY NEVER EXCEED THOSE IN ITS ORIGINAL "DIM" STATEMENT.

RE-DIMENSIONING

AFTER LINE 120 OPPOSITE, ARRAY B(,) IS *RE-DIMENSIONED* TO BE THE SAME AS ARRAY C(,). IT WOULD NOW BE WRONG TO HAVE :

```
130    LET  B(2,4) = 13
```

BECAUSE B(2,4) HAS CEASED TO EXIST. IN SPITE OF THIS SOME *BASICS* WOULD FAIL TO REPORT AN ERROR AND WOULD DO SOMETHING WITH UNPREDICTABLE RESULTS ⇄ THE 13 APPEARING PHANTOM-LIKE IN SOME OTHER LOCATION.

IT IS STILL ALLOWABLE TO HAVE :

```
140    MAT   B = A
```

EVEN THOUGH A(,) STILL HAS 3 ROWS & 4 COLUMNS WHEREAS B(,) CURRENTLY HAS ONLY 2 ROWS & 3 COLUMNS. A "MAT" INSTRUCTION (UNLIKE THE ORDINARY "LET" INSTRUCTION) RE-DIMENSIONS B(,) GIVING IT CURRENT DIMENSIONS OF 3 ROWS & 4 COLUMNS *ONCE AGAIN.*

IN GENERAL *BASIC* RE-DIMENSIONS AN ARRAY ON THE LEFT OF THE EQUALS SIGN ACCORDING TO CURRENT DIMENSIONS OF ARRAYS ON THE RIGHT *AS LONG AS THE ORIGINAL SIZE GIVEN IN THE "DIM" STATEMENT IS NOT EXCEEDED.* (THAT IS WHY LINE 110 OPPOSITE IS WRONG BUT 140 ABOVE IS CORRECT.)

THERE IS, HOWEVER, A COMPLICATION : MOST *BASICS* SEEM TO INTERPRET *"ORIGINAL SIZE"* AS MEANING THE TOTAL NUMBER OF ELEMENTS IN THE ORIGINAL ARRAY : THUS IF P(1,16) APPEARED IN THE "DIM" STATEMENT, P(,) COULD BECOME, THROUGH RE-DIMENSIONING, A SQUARE ARRAY OF FOUR ROWS AND FOUR COLUMNS. THIS IS NOT NICE. IT IS BETTER AND SAFER TO CONSIDER *EACH* DIMENSION AS AN INDIVIDUAL LIMIT OF RE-DIMENSION--ING ⇄ THUS P(1,16) IN THE ORIGINAL "DIM" STATEMENT MAY ATTAIN ANY NUMBER OF COLUMNS UP TO 16, BUT NEVER MORE THAN ONE ROW. IF YOU *PLAN* TO HAVE P(,) CHANGE FROM ONE ROW OF 16 ELEMENTS TO FOUR ROWS OF 4 ELEMENTS THEN YOU SHOULD DECLARE P(4,16) IN THE "DIM" STATEMENT.

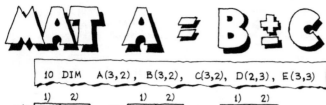

MAT A = B ± C

	10 DIM A(3,2), B(3,2), C(3,2), D(2,3), E(3,3)

	1)	2)
A(1,	4·3	0
A(2,	8·5	4
A(3,	9·4	4·3

	1)	2)
B(1,	1·5	-2·7
B(2,	3·6	7·8
B(3,	8·4	4·3

	1)	2)
C(1,	2·8	2·7
C(2,	4·9	-3·8
C(3,	1	0

	1)	2)	3)
D(1,			
D(2,			

	1)	2)	3)
E(1,			
E(2,			
E(3,			

SUPPOSE YOU WANT EACH ELEMENT OF ARRAY A( ) TO BE THE SUM (OR DIFFERENCE) OF THE TWO CORRESPONDING ELEMENTS IN ARRAYS B( ) AND C( ). YOU COULD ACHIEVE THIS AS FOLLOWS :

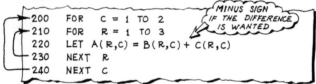

```
200    FOR   C = 1 TO 2
210    FOR   R = 1 TO 3
220    LET A(R,C) = B(R,C) + C(R,C)
230    NEXT  R
240    NEXT  C
```

> MINUS SIGN IF THE DIFFERENCE IS WANTED

BUT YOU COULD DO THE WHOLE THING WITH A SINGLE "MAT" INSTRUCTION LIKE THIS :

```
100    MAT    A = B + C
```

> OR MINUS

ARRAYS B( ) AND C( ) WOULD BE UNDISTURBED : ARRAY A( ) WOULD END UP AS SHOWN AT THE TOP OF THIS PAGE.

NOTICE THAT A, B & C ON LINE 100 HAVE NOTHING TO DO WITH THE ORDINARY VARIABLES A, B & C : THE WORD "MAT" TELLS *BASIC* YOU MEAN *ARRAYS* A( ), B( ) & C( ).

IF THE *CURRENT* DIMENSIONS OF THE TWO ARRAYS NAMED ON THE RIGHT OF THE EQUALS SIGN ARE NOT IDENTICAL THEN *BASIC* REFUSES TO OBEY THIS INSTRUCTION.

```
110    MAT    A = B + D
```

> DIM B(3,2) VS D(2,3)

THE ARRAY NAMED ON THE LEFT OF THE EQUALS SIGN MUST HAVE
DIMENSIONS AT LEAST AS GREAT AS THE *CURRENT* DIMENSIONS OF THE
ARRAYS NAMED ON THE RIGHT. THUS LINE 130 BELOW IS WRONG;
LINE 140 IS ALLOWED BUT WOULD CAUSE *BASIC* TO RE-DIMENSION
ARRAY E(,) SO THAT IT HAD 3 ROWS AND 2 COLUMNS; IT WOULD
THEN BE A MISTAKE TO REFER TO E(3,3). IMPLICATIONS OF
RE-DIMENSIONING ARE DISCUSSED ON PAGE 79.

```
130  MAT   D = B + C
140  MAT   E = B + C
150  LET   E(3,3) = 13
```

IN SOME (BUT *NOT* ALL) *BASICS* YOU ARE ALLOWED TO HAVE THE
NAME OF AN ARRAY ON BOTH SIDES OF THE EQUALS SIGN; FOR
THE SAKE OF "PORTABILITY" DON'T DO IT.

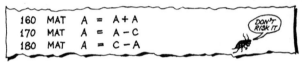

```
160  MAT   A = A + A
170  MAT   A = A - C
180  MAT   A = C - A
```

DON'T
RISK IT

THE FORM OF THIS INSTRUCTION MAY NOT BE VARIED. DON'T TRY
ADDING EXTRA SIGNS AND LETTERS.

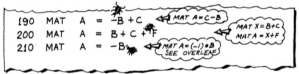

```
190  MAT   A = -B + C    ←  MAT A = C - B
200  MAT   A = B + C + F        MAT X = B + C
                                MAT A = X + F
210  MAT   A = -B        ←  MAT A = (-1)*B
                            SEE OVERLEAF
```

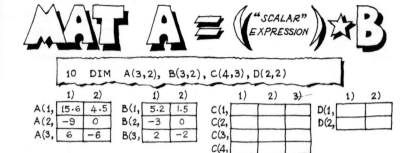

	1)	2)		1)	2)		1)	2)	3)		1)	2)
A(1,	15.6	4.5	B(1,	5.2	1.5	C(1,				D(1,		
A(2,	-9	0	B(2,	-3	0	C(2,				D(2,		
A(3,	6	-6	B(3,	2	-2	C(3,						
						C(4,						

10   DIM   A(3,2), B(3,2), C(4,3), D(2,2)

ＳUPPOSE YOU WANT EVERY ELEMENT OF ARRAY A(,) TO BE THREE TIMES THE VALUE OF THE CORRESPONDING ELEMENT IN ARRAY B(,). YOU CAN ACHIEVE THIS FAIRLY SIMPLY AS FOLLOWS :

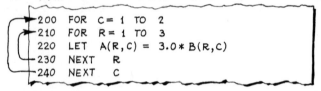

```
200   FOR  C = 1 TO 2
210   FOR  R = 1 TO 3
220   LET  A(R,C) = 3.0 * B(R,C)
230   NEXT   R
240   NEXT   C
```

BUT YOU COULD DO THE WHOLE THING WITH A SINGLE "MAT" STATEMENT LIKE THIS :

```
100   MAT   A = (3.0) * B
```

ARRAY B(,) WOULD REMAIN UNDISTURBED AND A(,) WOULD NOW BE AS SHOWN AT THE TOP OF THIS PAGE. EVERY ELEMENT HAS BEEN SCALED BY THE *SCALAR* (*i.e. NON*-VECTOR *or NON*-MATRIX) EXPRESSION IN BRACKETS.

Ｎ OTICE THAT A & B ON LINE 100 HAVE NOTHING TO DO WITH THE SIMPLE VARIABLES A & B ; THE WORD "MAT" TELLS *BASIC* YOU MEAN *ARRAYS* A(,) & B(,). BUT *INSIDE* THE BRACKETS A & B *WOULD* BE SIMPLE VARIABLES : LINE 130 BELOW WOULD HAVE EXACTLY THE SAME EFFECT AS LINE 100 ABOVE ; (A/B) REPRESENTS THE SCALAR QUANTITY (3.0).

```
110   LET  A = 6
120   LET  B = 2
130   MAT  A = (A/B) * B
```

THE ARRAY NAMED ON THE LEFT OF THE EQUALS SIGN MUST HAVE
DIMENSIONS IN THE "DIM" STATEMENT AT LEAST AS BIG AS THE
CURRENT DIMENSIONS OF THE ARRAY NAMED ON THE RIGHT.
THUS LINE 140 BELOW IS WRONG: LINE 150 IS ALLOWED BUT
WOULD CAUSE *BASIC* TO RE-DIMENSION ARRAY C(,) SO THAT IT
HAD 3 ROWS AND 2 COLUMNS : IT WOULD THEN BE A MISTAKE
TO REFER TO C(4,2). IMPLICATIONS OF RE-DIMENSIONING
ARE DISCUSSED ON PAGE 79.

```
140   MAT  D =  (0.5) * B
150   MAT  C =  (-1) * B
160   LET  C(4,2) =  13
```

IN SOME (*NOT* ALL) *BASICS* YOU ARE ALLOWED TO NAME THE
SAME ARRAY ON BOTH SIDES OF THE EQUALS SIGN : FOR THE
SAKE OF "PORTABILITY" DON'T DO IT:

```
170   MAT  A = (-X) * A
```

DON'T
DO IT!

THE EXPRESSION IN BRACKETS MAY BE AS COMPLICATED AS YOU
LIKE AS LONG AS IT REPRESENTS A SINGLE SCALAR VALUE:

```
180   MAT  A = (-X + SQR(3 * B(2*I,J))) * B
```

THE FORM OF THIS INSTRUCTION IS STRICTLY AS SHOWN IN THE
HEADING OPPOSITE. SOME ERRORS OF FORM ARE ILLUSTRATED
BELOW:

```
185   LET  X = 3
190   MAT  A = X * B          THIS IS THE FORM FOR "MATRIX
                              MULTIPLICATION. SEE PAGE 88
192   MAT  A = -(X) * B        MAT A = (-X) * B
194   MAT  A = (X) * (Y) * B   MAT A = (X*Y) * B
196   MAT  A = B * (X)         MAT A = (X) * B
```

MAT A = TRN(B)

```
10   DIM   A(3,2), B(2,3), C(3,3), D(2,2)
```

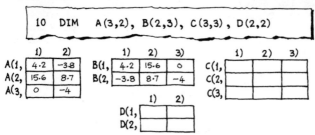

	1)	2)
A(1,	4·2	-3·8
A(2,	15·6	8·7
A(3,	0	-4

	1)	2)	3)
B(1,	4·2	15·6	0
B(2,	-3·8	8·7	-4

	1)	2)	3)
C(1,			
C(2,			
C(3,			

	1)	2)
D(1,		
D(2,		

SUPPOSE YOU WANT THE *ROWS* OF ARRAY A(,) TO BE THE SAME AS THE *COLUMNS* OF ARRAY B(,) ⟷ IN OTHER WORDS YOU WANT A(,) TO BE THE *TRANSPOSE* OF B(,). YOU COULD COPY THE ELEMENTS ONE BY ONE LIKE THIS:

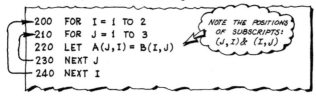

```
200   FOR I = 1 TO 2
210   FOR J = 1 TO 3
220   LET A(J,I) = B(I,J)
230   NEXT J
240   NEXT I
```

NOTE THE POSITIONS OF SUBSCRIPTS: (J,I) & (I,J)

BUT YOU COULD DO THE WHOLE THING WITH A SINGLE "MAT" INSTRUCTION LIKE THIS:

```
100   MAT   A = TRN(B)
```

ARRAY B(,) WOULD BE UNDISTURBED; ARRAY A(,) WOULD END UP AS SHOWN AT THE TOP OF THIS PAGE.

NOTICE THAT A & B ON LINE 100 HAVE NOTHING TO DO WITH THE SIMPLE VARIABLES A & B; THE WORD "MAT" TELLS *BASIC* YOU MEAN *ARRAYS* A(,) & B(,).

THE ARRAY NAMED ON THE LEFT OF THE EQUALS SIGN MUST HAVE DIMENSIONS IN ITS "DIM" STATEMENT AT LEAST AS BIG AS THE *CURRENT* DIMENSIONS OF THE ARRAY NAMED ON THE RIGHT. THUS LINE 110 OPPOSITE IS WRONG; LINE 120 IS ALLOWED BUT WOULD CAUSE *BASIC* TO RE-DIMENSION ARRAY C(,) SO THAT IT HAD *THREE* ROWS AND *TWO* COLUMNS (NB. NOT 2 ROWS & 3 COLUMNS) AND IT WOULD THEN BE A MISTAKE TO REFER TO C(3,3).

84

IMPLICATIONS OF RE-DIMENSIONING ARE DISCUSSED ON PAGE 79.

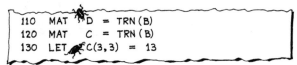

```
110   MAT   D = TRN(B)
120   MAT   C = TRN(B)
130   LET   C(3,3) = 13
```

YOU MAY NOT NAME THE SAME ARRAY ON BOTH SIDES OF THE EQUALS SIGN: IN OTHER WORDS YOU MAY NOT TRANSPOSE A MATRIX ON TOP OF ITSELF:

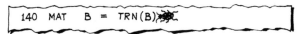

```
140   MAT   B = TRN(B)
```

BUT SOME *BASICS* DO ALLOW THIS. AS AN EXERCISE IT MIGHT AMUSE YOU TO WRITE A ROUTINE FOR REPLACING AN ARRAY BY THE TRANSPOSE OF ITSELF ⟿ BUT WITHOUT COPYING IT FIRST TO SOME OTHER ARRAY (IN OTHER WORDS YOU SHOULD TRANSPOSE THE ARRAY " IN-SITU "). IT IS TRICKY BUT NOT IMPOSSIBLE.

TRANSPOSITION IS A USEFUL OPERATION IN MATRIX ALGEBRA: IN PARTICULAR FOR TRANSFORMING COORDINATES FROM ONE SET OF AXES TO ANOTHER. THE SIMPLEST EXAMPLE OF THIS IS ILLUSTRATED BELOW.

THE COORDINATES OF POINT **P** RELATIVE TO U & V ARE u & v RESPECTIVELY. WHAT ARE THE COORDINATES OF **P** RELATIVE TO AXES X & Y **?**

USING TRIGONOMETRY:

$$x = u\cos\theta - v\sin\theta$$
$$y = u\sin\theta + v\cos\theta$$

WHICH MAY BE WRITTEN IN MATRIX FORM AS BELOW:

$$\begin{bmatrix} x \\ y \end{bmatrix} = \begin{bmatrix} \cos\theta & -\sin\theta \\ \sin\theta & \cos\theta \end{bmatrix} \begin{bmatrix} u \\ v \end{bmatrix} \quad \dots(1)$$

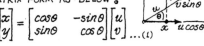

ALSO USING TRIGONOMETRY IT IS JUST AS SIMPLE TO FIND A PAIR OF EQUATIONS YIELDING u AND v IN TERMS OF x AND y :

$$\begin{bmatrix} u \\ v \end{bmatrix} = \begin{bmatrix} \cos\theta & \sin\theta \\ -\sin\theta & \cos\theta \end{bmatrix} \begin{bmatrix} x \\ y \end{bmatrix} \quad \dots(2)$$

NOTICE THAT EACH OF THESE SQUARE MATRICES IS THE TRANSPOSE OF THE OTHER.

IT IS GENERALLY TRUE OF ORTHOGONAL AXIS TRANSFORMATIONS THAT TO REVERSE THE TRANSFORMATION YOU SIMPLY *TRANSPOSE* THE TRANSFORMING MATRIX. IN TEXT BOOKS MATRICES ARE OFTEN INDICATED BY LETTERS IN BOLD TYPE AND TRANSPOSITION BY A *PRIME*. THE TWO EQUATIONS ABOVE MIGHT BE SHOWN AS: $\mathbf{X = TU}$ AND $\mathbf{U = T'X}$.

MAT A = ZER

```
10   DIM   A(3,4) , B(2,3)
```

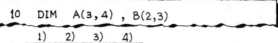

	1)	2)	3)	4)
A(1,	0	0	0	0
A(2,	0	0	0	0
A(3,	0	0	0	0

	1)	2)	3)
B(1,	1	1	1
B(2,	1	1	1

YOU MAY MAKE ALL ELEMENTS OF AN ARRAY ZERO LIKE THIS:

```
200   FOR   R = 1 TO 3
210   FOR   C = 1 TO 4
220   LET   A(R,C) = 0
230   NEXT  C
240   NEXT  R
```

BUT YOU COULD DO THE WHOLE THING WITH A SINGLE "MAT"
INSTRUCTION LIKE THIS:

```
100   MAT   A = ZER
```

WHERE "ZER" IS SIMPLY A WORD SHORT FOR ZERO, AND LETTER
A HAS NOTHING TO DO WITH THE SIMPLE VARIABLE A. THE WORD
"MAT" TELLS *BASIC* YOU MEAN ARRAY A(,).

TAKE **CARE** WITH THIS INSTRUCTION 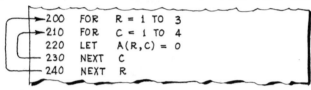 AND WITH "CON" AND
"IDN" DESCRIBED BELOW. THE ARRAY NAMED ON THE LEFT OF THE
EQUALS SIGN IS ASSUMED BY SOME *BASICS* TO RETAIN ITS
CURRENT DIMENSIONS WHICH MAY BE SMALLER THAN THOSE IN
ITS "DIM" STATEMENT. SO UNLESS THIS IS THE VERY FIRST "MAT"
INSTRUCTION TO BE OBEYED IT IS SAFER TO USE THE ALTERNATIVE
FORM:

*EXPRESSIONS
ALLOWED HERE*

```
110   MAT   A = ZER(2,3)
```

WHICH HAS THE EFFECT OF RE-DIMENSIONING THE ARRAY NAMED ON
THE LEFT OF THE EQUALS SIGN AS WELL AS SETTING ITS ELEMENTS
TO ZERO. IMPLICATIONS OF RE-DIMENSIONING ARE DISCUSSED ON
PAGE 79. IF *YOU* DO USE EXPRESSIONS FOR DIMENSIONS,
MAKE CERTAIN (PERHAPS USING "INT") THAT YOUR EXPRESSIONS
YIELD INTEGRAL RESULTS. SOME *BASICS* USE THE *NEAREST*
INTEGER TO THE RESULT BUT OTHERS TAKE THE *INTEGRAL PART*
OF THE RESULT.

86

THE ONLY DIFFERENCE BETWEEN THIS INSTRUCTION AND "MAT A = ZER"
IS THAT THE RESULTING ARRAY IS FULL OF 1'S RATHER THAN 0'S.

```
120    MAT  B =  CON(2,3)
```

"CON" IS SHORT FOR *CONSTANT*. YOU CAN SET ALL ELEMENTS TO
ANY CONSTANT IN TWO "MAT" INSTRUCTIONS.

```
130    MAT  A =  CON(2,3)
140    MAT  B =  (-5)*A
```
ALL ELEMENTS OF B(,) SET TO −5

"IDN" IS SHORT FOR *IDENTITY*. (AN "IDENTITY MATRIX" IN
MATRIX ALGEBRA IS ANALOGOUS TO *UNITY* IN ORDINARY ALGEBRA:
THIS IS DEMONSTRATED ON PAGE 91.) THE IDENTITY MATRIX
HAS 1'S ON THE *DIAGONAL* (WHERE ROW & COLUMN SUBSCRIPTS
ARE EQUAL) AND 0'S *OFF THE DIAGONAL* (WHERE SUBSCRIPTS
ARE *UN*EQUAL). HERE IS ONE WAY TO PROGRAM IT :

	1)	2)	3)
A(1,	1	0	0
A(2,	0	1	0
A(3,	0	0	1

```
200    FOR  R = 1  TO 3
210    FOR  C = 1  TO 3
220    LET  A(R,C)=1-ABS(SGN(R-C))
230    NEXT C
240    NEXT R
```

BUT YOU CAN DO IT WITH A SINGLE "MAT" INSTRUCTION :

```
150    MAT  A =  IDN(3,3)
```
IDENTITY MATRICES ARE ALWAYS SQUARE

YOU MAY LEAVE OFF THE DIMENSIONS AND HAVE JUST "MAT A=IDN"
BUT ONLY IF THE *CURRENT* DIMENSIONS OF A(,) ARE EQUAL.

YOU MAY ALSO HAVE *EXPRESSIONS* FOR DIMENSIONS INSTEAD OF
WRITTEN INTEGERS AS ABOVE. FOR EXAMPLE "MAT A=IDN(X,2*Y+3)"
BUT THE RESULTS OF BOTH EXPRESSIONS MUST BE THE SAME WHEN
BASIC EVALUATES THEM BECAUSE THERE IS NO SUCH THING AS A
NON-SQUARE IDENTITY MATRIX. FURTHERMORE YOU SHOULD
MAKE CERTAIN YOUR EXPRESSIONS CAN ONLY YIELD INTEGRAL
RESULTS FOR THE REASONS GIVEN OPPOSITE.

MAT R ≡ A ☆ B

HERE IS A SIMPLE ILLUSTRATION OF "MATRIX MULTIPLICATION" WITHOUT THE USE OF A "MAT" INSTRUCTION.

THERE ARE 3 SALES-PEOPLE EACH SELLING 4 PRODUCTS; THEIR WEEKLY ACHIEVEMENT IS TABULATED LIKE THIS:

PERSON / SALESMAN	PRODUCT MAGLETS	SCROPERS	GIMPLES	NUCKERS
MR. HOGG	5	2	0	10
MS. BURNTBRA	3	5	2	5
M. CHAUVIN	20	0	0	0

WEEKLY SALES: FORM $A(3,4)$

THE LIST OF PRICES AND SALES COMMISSIONS (IN MONEY; NOT AS A PERCENTAGE) IS TABULATED LIKE THIS:

PRICE LIST: $B(4,2)$

PRODUCT	PRICE	COMMISSION
MAGLETS	1.50	0.20
SCROPERS	2.80	0.40
GIMPLES	5.00	1.00
NUCKERS	2.00	0.50

"INNER PRODUCTS"

SO THE MONEY BROUGHT IN IS:

MR. HOGG	$5 \times 1.50 + 2 \times 2.80 + 0 \times 5.00 + 10 \times 2.00$	$= 33.10$
MS. BURNTBRA	$3 \times 1.50 + 5 \times 2.80 + 2 \times 5.00 + 5 \times 2.00$	$= 38.50$
M. CHAUVIN	$20 \times 1.50 + 0 \times 2.80 + 0 \times 5.00 + 0 \times 2.00$	$= 30.00$

AND THE COMMISSIONS EARNED ARE:

MR. HOGG	$5 \times 0.20 + 2 \times 0.40 + 0 \times 1.00 + 10 \times 0.50$	$= 6.80$
MS. BURNTBRA	$3 \times 0.20 + 5 \times 0.40 + 2 \times 1.00 + 5 \times 0.50$	$= 7.10$
M. CHAUVIN	$20 \times 0.20 + 0 \times 0.40 + 0 \times 1.00 + 0 \times 0.50$	$= 4.00$

IF THIS WERE PUT ON THE COMPUTER THE WEEKLY SALES ACHIEVEMENT COULD BE STORED IN ARRAY A(,), THE PRICE LIST RESIDING IN ARRAY B(,), AND THE RESULTS SENT TO ARRAY R(,) PRIOR TO PRINTING. THE PROGRAM MIGHT CONTAIN THE FOLLOWING CODE:

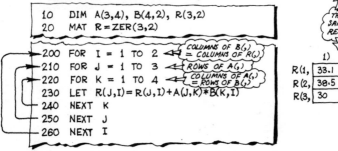

```
10    DIM A(3,4), B(4,2), R(3,2)
20    MAT R = ZER(3,2)

200   FOR I = 1 TO 2      ← COLUMNS OF B( , ) = COLUMNS OF R( , )
210   FOR J = 1 TO 3      ← ROWS OF A( , )
220   FOR K = 1 TO 4      ← COLUMNS OF A( , ) = ROWS OF B( , )
230   LET R(J,I)=R(J,I)+A(J,K)*B(K,I)
240   NEXT K
250   NEXT J
260   NEXT I
```

THE SAME RESULTS

	1)	2)
R(1,	33.1	6.8
R(2,	38.5	7.1
R(3,	30	4

THE COLUMNS OF R(,) WOULD THEN CONTAIN THE "LONG-HAND" RESULTS ABOVE.

THE CODE FROM LINE 200 TO 260 COULD BE REPLACED BY THE SINGLE "MAT" INSTRUCTION:

```
100    MAT  R = A * B
```

THE ROWS OF A(,) ARE CUMULATIVELY MULTIPLIED BY THE COLUMNS OF B(,). WHAT GOES INTO $R(r,c)$? ANSWER: THE INNER PRODUCT OF THE rth ROW OF A(,) AND THE cth COLUMN OF B(,).

FOR THIS "MAT" INSTRUCTION TO WORK AT ALL IT IS IMPERATIVE FOR ARRAYS TO HAVE CURRENT DIMENSIONS MAKING THEM "CONFORMABLE".

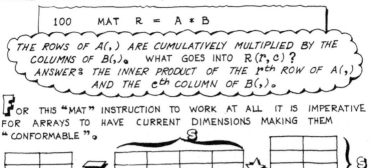

$$R(r,c) = A(r,s) ☆ B(s,c)$$

N° OF ROWS IN RESULT — SAME "INSIDE" DIMENSION — N° OF COLUMNS IN RESULT

IN THE EXAMPLE OPPOSITE A(,) HAS DIMENSIONS (3,4) AND B(,) HAS DIMENSIONS (4,2), SO THE "4" ON THE "INSIDE" MAKES A(,) & B(,) CONFORMABLE. BUT IT WOULD BE TOTALLY WRONG TO HAVE:

```
110    MAT  R = B * A
```

IN ORDINARY ALGEBRA $a \times b = b \times a$ ⟺ MULTIPLICATION IS "COMMUTATIVE" ⟺ BUT IN MATRIX ALGEBRA $b \times a$ MAY NOT EVEN *EXIST*. IN THIS EXAMPLE LINE 110 IS COMPLETE NONSENSE.

PROVIDED THAT A(,) & B(,) *ARE* CONFORMABLE, ARRAY R(,) IS RE-DIMENSIONED TO HAVE AS MANY ROWS AS THE CURRENT *FIRST* DIMENSION OF A(,) AND AS MANY COLUMNS AS THE CURRENT *SECOND* DIMENSION OF B(,). IF THESE DIMENSIONS EXCEED THOSE IN THE "DIM" STATEMENT FOR R(,) THEN *BASIC* REPORTS AN ERROR AND STOPS WORK. OTHER IMPLICATIONS OF RE-DIMENSIONING ARE DISCUSSED ON PAGE 79.

YOU ARE NOT ALLOWED TO VARY THE SIMPLE FORM OF THIS INSTRUCTION AND YOU MAY NOT NAME THE SAME ARRAY ON BOTH SIDES OF THE EQUALS SIGN.

```
120    MAT  P = A * P
```

FOR AN ORDINARY ALGEBRAIC EQUATION:

$$4.5 X = 37$$

THE SOLUTION IS:

$$X = (4.5)^{-1} \times 37$$
$$= 0.2222 \times 37$$
$$= 8.222$$

THE PROCEDURE IS TO "INVERT" THE COEFFICIENT OF X AND MULTIPLY BY THE RIGHT-HAND SIDE (*RHS*). NOTICE THAT THE ORIGINAL COEFFICIENT, 4.5, MULTIPLIED BY ITS "INVERSE", 0.2222, IS 0.9999.... (IDEALLY EXACTLY 1).

IN *MATRIX* ALGEBRA THERE IS AN ANALOGOUS APPROACH TO *SIMULTANEOUS* EQUATIONS. CONSIDER THESE THREE:

$$15X + 10Y + 5Z = 3.1$$
$$12X + 24Y + 8Z = 4.5$$
$$6X \qquad + 36Z = 6.3$$

THEY MAY BE WRITTEN IN MATRIX FORM LIKE THIS:

$$\begin{bmatrix} 15 & 10 & 5 \\ 12 & 24 & 8 \\ 6 & 0 & 36 \end{bmatrix} * \begin{bmatrix} X \\ Y \\ Z \end{bmatrix} = \begin{bmatrix} 3.1 \\ 4.5 \\ 6.3 \end{bmatrix}$$

(IF YOU FORM THE INNER PRODUCT OF ROW 1 OF THE FIRST MATRIX AND COLUMN 1 OF THE SECOND YOU GET $15 \times X + 10 \times Y + 5 \times Z$ *etc.* JUST AS THE INNER PRODUCTS ARE SET OUT ON PAGE 88.)

THE SOLUTION OF THE EQUATIONS IS:

$$\begin{bmatrix} X \\ Y \\ Z \end{bmatrix} = \begin{bmatrix} 15 & 10 & 5 \\ 12 & 24 & 8 \\ 6 & 0 & 36 \end{bmatrix}^{-1} * \begin{bmatrix} 3.1 \\ 4.5 \\ 6.3 \end{bmatrix}$$

WHERE THE " -1 " AS A SUPERSCRIPT TO THE MATRIX DENOTES THE "INVERSE" OF THAT MATRIX, WHICH (AS WILL BE SHOWN) WORKS OUT LIKE THIS:

$$\begin{bmatrix} X \\ Y \\ Z \end{bmatrix} = \begin{bmatrix} .1029 & -.0429 & -.00476 \\ -.0457 & .0607 & -.00714 \\ -.0171 & .00714 & .0286 \end{bmatrix} * \begin{bmatrix} 3.1 \\ 4.5 \\ 6.3 \end{bmatrix}$$

FROM WHICH YOU CAN GET ANSWERS FOR *ANY* RIGHT-HAND SIDE BY MATRIX MULTIPLICATION. FOR EXAMPLE, TO GET Y (ROW 2, COLUMN 1):
$$Y = -0.0457 \times 3.1 + 0.0607 \times 4.5 - 0.00714 \times 6.3 = 0.4598$$

TO COMPLETE THE ANALOGY WITH ORDINARY ALGEBRA, MULTIPLY THE
ORIGINAL MATRIX OF COEFFICIENTS BY ITS INVERSE :

$$\begin{bmatrix} 15 & 10 & 5 \\ 12 & 24 & 8 \\ 6 & 0 & 36 \end{bmatrix} * \begin{bmatrix} \cdot1029 & -\cdot0429 & -\cdot00476 \\ -\cdot0457 & \cdot0607 & -\cdot00714 \\ -\cdot0171 & \cdot00714 & \cdot0286 \end{bmatrix} = \begin{bmatrix} 1\cdot001 & -\cdot0008 & -\cdot0088 \\ \cdot0012 & \cdot9991 & \cdot00032 \\ \cdot0018 & -\cdot00036 & 1\cdot001 \end{bmatrix}$$

GIVING A MATRIX VERY NEAR TO THE *IDENTITY* MATRIX ⇌ A SORT OF
"MATRIX UNITY". (IDEALLY THE ANSWER SHOULD BE PRECISELY THIS BUT
WE WORKED TO ONLY 4 SIGNIFICANT FIGURES.)

𝒮O YOU CAN GET THE INVERSE SHOWN ABOVE BY SOLVING 3 SIMUL-
TANEOUS EQUATIONS USING THE COLUMNS OF THE IDENTITY MATRIX AS RIGHT-
HAND SIDES ⇌ EFFECTIVELY "DIVIDING" *MATRIX UNITY* BY THE COEFFICIENTS
⇌ OR "INVERTING" THE MATRIX OF COEFFICIENTS.

$$\begin{array}{rrrrrr} 15\times X & + & 10\times Y + 5\times Z = & 1 & \text{THEN } 0 & \text{THEN } 0 \\ 12\times X & + & 24\times Y + 8\times Z = & 0 & 1 & 0 \\ 6\times X & + & 0\times Y + 36\times Z = & 0 & 0 & 1 \end{array}$$

WE DO THIS AS WE DID AT SCHOOL BUT PERHAPS IN A MORE RIGIDLY-
ORDERED SEQUENCE. FIRST ELIMINATE COEFFICIENTS OF X IN EQUATIONS
2 AND 3. MULTIPLY EQ.2 BY 15, DIVIDE THROUGH BY 12, AND
SUBTRACT THIS SCALED EQUATION FROM EQ.1 THUS GIVING A NEW EQ.2.
SIMILARLY FORM A NEW EQ.3 BY MULTIPLYING EQ.3 BY 15, DIVIDING
THROUGH BY 6, AND SUBTRACTING FROM EQ.1.

$$\begin{array}{lrrrrrr} & 15\times X & + & 10\times Y + 5\times Z = & 1 & 0 & 0 \\ EQ2 = EQ1 - (15/12)\times EQ2 \ldots & 0\times X & - & 20\times Y - 5\times Z = & 1 & -1\cdot25 & 0 \\ EQ3 = EQ1 - (15/6)\times EQ3 \ldots & 0\times X & + & 10\times Y - 85\times Z = & 1 & 0 & -2\cdot5 \end{array}$$

NOW ELIMINATE THE COEFFICIENT OF Y IN NEW EQUATION 3. MULTIPLY EQ.3
BY −20, DIVIDE THROUGH BY 10, AND SUBTRACT FROM EQ.2.

$$\begin{array}{lrrrrrr} & 15\times X & + & 10\times Y + 5\times Z = & 1 & 0 & 0 \\ & 0\times X & - & 20\times Y - 5\times Z = & 1 & -1\cdot25 & 0 \\ EQ3 = EQ2 - (-20/10)\times EQ3 \ldots & 0\times X & + & 0\times Y - 175\times Z = & 3 & -1\cdot25 & -5 \end{array}$$

THE ORIGINAL MATRIX OF COEFFICIENTS NOW HAS ALL ELEMENTS BELOW THE
DIAGONAL EQUAL TO ZERO. SO NOW "BACK SUBSTITUTE" STARTING AT
EQUATION 3 AND WORKING BACK TO EQUATION 1.

THE ONLY UNKNOWN IN EQ.3 IS Z, SO DIVIDE *RH*-SIDES BY −175 :

$$Z = -\cdot0171 \quad \cdot00714 \quad \cdot0286$$

NOW FROM EACH *RHS* OF EQ.2 SUBTRACT (−5) TIMES THE CORRESPONDING
VALUE OF Z, AND DIVIDE BY THE COEFFICIENT OF Y WHICH IS (−20)
(*e.g.* THE FIRST IS $[1-(-5)\times(-\cdot0171)] \div (-20) = -\cdot0457$).

$$Y = -\cdot0457 \quad \cdot0607 \quad -\cdot00714$$

FINALLY, FROM EACH *RHS* OF EQ.1 SUBTRACT 5 TIMES THE CORRESPONDING VALUE OF
Z, 10 TIMES THE CORRESPONDING VALUE OF Y, AND DIVIDE BY 15
(*e.g.* THE FIRST IS $[1-5*(-\cdot0171)-10\times(-\cdot0457)] \div 15 = \cdot1029$).

$$X = \cdot1029 \quad -\cdot0429 \quad -\cdot00476$$

THESE ARE THE 3 ROWS OF THE INVERSE ⇌ PRODUCED IN REVERSE ORDER.

MAT A = INV(B)

	10	DIM	A(3,3),	B(3,3),	I(3,3)

	1)	2)	3)
A(1,			
A(2,			
A(3,			

	1)	2)	3)
B(1,	15	10	5
B(2,	12	24	8
B(3,	6	0	36

HERE IS A ROUTINE TO INVERT A MATRIX OF DIMENSIONS
N BY N STORED AS AN ARRAY B(,): THE INVERSE IS
BUILT UP IN A(,). THE METHOD USED IS EXPLAINED BY THE
EXAMPLE ON THE PREVIOUS DOUBLE PAGE.

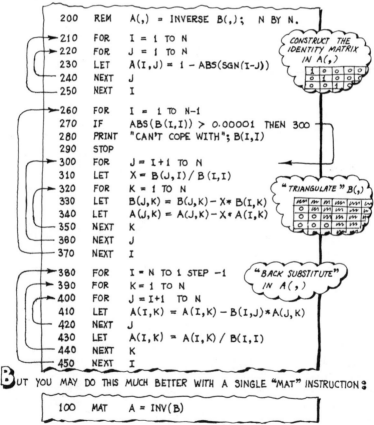

```
200   REM    A(,) = INVERSE B(,);  N BY N.
210   FOR    I = 1 TO N
220   FOR    J = 1 TO N
230   LET    A(I,J) = 1 - ABS(SGN(I-J))
240   NEXT   J
250   NEXT   I

260   FOR    I = 1 TO N-1
270   IF     ABS(B(I,I)) > 0.00001 THEN 300
280   PRINT  "CAN'T COPE WITH"; B(I,I)
290   STOP
300   FOR    J = I+1 TO N
310   LET    X = B(J,I) / B(I,I)
320   FOR    K = 1 TO N
330   LET    B(J,K) = B(J,K) - X * B(I,K)
340   LET    A(J,K) = A(J,K) - X * A(I,K)
350   NEXT   K
360   NEXT   J
370   NEXT   I

380   FOR    I = N TO 1 STEP -1
390   FOR    K = 1 TO N
400   FOR    J = I+1 TO N
410   LET    A(I,K) = A(I,K) - B(I,J) * A(J,K)
420   NEXT   J
430   LET    A(I,K) = A(I,K) / B(I,I)
440   NEXT   K
450   NEXT   I
```

CONSTRUCT THE IDENTITY MATRIX IN A(,)

"TRIANGULATE" B(,)

"BACK SUBSTITUTE" IN A(,)

BUT YOU MAY DO THIS MUCH BETTER WITH A SINGLE "MAT" INSTRUCTION:

```
100   MAT    A = INV(B)
```

IF THE MATRIX HAS NO INVERSE ((IF IT IS "SINGULAR")) THEN SOME *BASICS* REPORT AN ERROR AND STOP EXECUTION ⁏ OTHERS DON'T REPORT AN ERROR BUT PROVIDE THE MEANS OF PICKING UP THE *DETERMINANT* OF THE MATRIX AS SHOWN BELOW. A ZERO DETERMINANT IMPLIES A SINGULAR MATRIX. ((A DETERMINANT IS *ILLUSTRATED* ON PAGE 43.))

```
110    LET  D = DET
120    IF   D > ·001  THEN  150          CARRY
130    PRINT "SINGULAR MATRIX"            ON
140    STOP
```

THE VALUE PROVIDED BY "DET" IS THE VALUE OF THE DETERMINANT OF THE MATRIX LAST INVERTED ((OR LAST ATTEMPTED)) BY YOUR PROGRAM. NOT ALL *BASICS*, HOWEVER, PROVIDE THE "DET" FUNCTION.

A *NON*-SQUARE MATRIX CAN HAVE NO INVERSE ➔ ATTEMPTS TO COMPUTE ONE ARE TREATED AS MISTAKES. AND MOST *BASICS* REFUSE TO REPLACE A MATRIX BY ITS OWN INVERSE.

```
150    MAT  A = CON(2,3)       NOT
                               SQUARE
160    MAT  B = INV(A)
                               SAME NAME
170    MAT  B = INV(B)         BOTH SIDES
```

YOU CAN JUDGE THE ACCURACY OF INVERSION BY PRINTING THE PRODUCT OF THE ORIGINAL MATRIX AND ITS INVERSE. BY DEFINITION THIS SHOULD BE THE IDENTITY MATRIX EXACTLY BUT USUALLY DIFFERS BECAUSE OF "ROUNDING" ERRORS AS PREVIOUSLY ILLUSTRATED USING FOUR SIGNIFICANT FIGURES.

```
180    MAT  A = INV(B)          "MAT PRINT"
                                IS DESCRIBED
190    MAT  I = B * A           ON PAGE 98
195    MAT  PRINT I
```

THE DIMENSIONS OF A(,) IN ITS "DIM" STATEMENT MUST BE AT LEAST AS BIG AS THE *CURRENT* DIMENSIONS OF B(,) AT LINE 180 ABOVE. IMPLICATIONS OF RE-DIMENSIONING ARE DISCUSSED ON PAGE 79.

THE ROUTINE FROM LINE 200 OPPOSITE DIFFERS IN ITS EFFECT FROM "MAT A = INV(B)". FIRST OF ALL IT MAKES A MESS OF ARRAY B(,) ⁏ THE "MAT" INSTRUCTION SHOULD *NOT* DO THIS. ((IF YOUR VERSION *DOES* MANGLE B(,) IT WILL BE EVIDENT WHEN YOU RUN THE TEST AT LINE 180 ABOVE.)) SECONDLY THE ROUTINE OPPOSITE ONLY WORKS WELL IF NUMBERS ON THE DIAGONAL OF B(,) ARE MUCH THE SAME SIZE AS ONE ANOTHER AND BIGGER THAN TERMS *OFF* THE DIAGONAL. ((IT WILL NOT WORK AT ALL IF B(1,1) IS ZERO.)) THE "MAT" INSTRUCTION SHOULD SELECT BEST DIVISORS ⁏ NOT SIMPLY USE DIAGONAL ELEMENTS AS DONE AT LINE 310 OPPOSITE FOR THE SAKE OF A SIMPLE ILLUSTRATION.

 **MAT READ**

THIS INSTRUCTION READS FROM THE SAME "DATA" STATEMENTS AS THE ORDINARY "READ".

```
10   DIM   A(2,3),  B(3,1),  C(1,3)
20   DATA  1.5, 2.3, 3.2, 4.6, 5.7, 6.5, 7.1
30   DATA  8.9, 9.0, 11.7, 12.6, 13, 14, 15
```

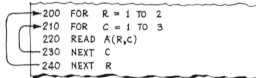

	1)	2)	3)
A(1,	1.5	2.3	3.2
A(2,	4.6	5.7	6.5

B(1,	7.1
B(2,	8.9
B(3,	9.0

	1)	2)	3)
C(1,	11.7	12.6	13

$\mathcal{S}$UPPOSE YOU WANT TO FILL ARRAY A(,) BY ROWS FROM THE QUEUE OF DATA STARTING ON LINE 20. YOU COULD DO IT LIKE THIS:

```
200   FOR   R = 1 TO 2
210   FOR   C = 1 TO 3
220   READ  A(R,C)
230   NEXT  C
240   NEXT  R
```

BUT YOU COULD DO THE WHOLE THING WITH A SINGLE "MAT" STATEMENT LIKE THIS:

```
100   MAT   READ  A
```
A(,) IS READ BY ROWS

IN FACT YOU MAY FILL ANY NUMBER OF ARRAYS (BY ROWS) USING A SINGLE "MAT" INSTRUCTION:

```
100   MAT   READ  A, B, C
```
ALWAYS COMMAS IN THIS LIST

THE ARRAYS A(,), B(,) & C(,) WOULD THEN BE AS SHOWN AT THE TOP OF THIS PAGE. NOTICE THE LETTERS A, B & C HAVE NOTHING TO DO WITH SIMPLE VARIABLES A, B & C.

$\left(\bullet\right)$N THE OTHER HAND YOU MAY *PARTIALLY* FILL ARRAYS BY SPECIFYING NEW DIMENSIONS IN THE "MAT" INSTRUCTION ⟵ AS LONG AS THEY ARE NO BIGGER THAN THOSE IN THE "DIM" STATEMENTS.

```
100   MAT   READ   A(2,2), B,  C(1,1)
```

	1)	2)
A(1,	1.5	2.3
A(2,	3.2	4.6

B(1,	5.7
B(2,	6.5
B(3,	7.1

	1)
C(1,	8.9

IF YOU OMIT DIMENSIONS FROM "MAT READ" THEN *BASIC* USES THE *CURRENT* DIMENSIONS OF THAT ARRAY ⟵ THESE MAY BE SMALLER THAN THOSE IN ITS "DIM" STATEMENT.

```
100    MAT    A = ZER(1,1)
110    MAT    READ    A
```

THUS THE INSTRUCTIONS ABOVE WOULD CAUSE JUST ONE
NUMBER TO BE READ INTO THE 1 BY 1 ARRAY A(,) .
IMPLICATIONS OF SUCH RE-DIMENSIONING ARE DISCUSSED ON PAGE 79.

YOU MAY HAVE VARIABLES OR EXPRESSIONS AS DIMENSIONS IN
THE "MAT" STATEMENT :

```
10    DIM      E(10,10)        DIMENSIONS
20    DATA     2, 3            AS DATA
30    DATA     1.1, 2.2, 3.3, 4.4, 5.5, 6.6
40    READ     R, C
50    MAT      READ    E(R,C)  EXPRESSIONS
                               ALLOWED HERE
```

BUT ALWAYS ENSURE (PERHAPS BY USING "INT") THAT THE EXPRESSIONS
YIELD INTEGRAL RESULTS BECAUSE SOME *BASICS* USE THE *NEAREST*
INTEGER TO THE RESULT AND OTHERS USE THE *INTEGRAL PART* .

THERE IS ONLY ONE QUEUE OF DATA IN THE "DATA" STATEMENTS
AND EACH "READ" OR "MAT READ" TAKES WHAT IT NEEDS WHEN
OBEYED. THE INSTRUCTION "RESTORE" TAKES THE PROGRAM
BACK TO THE BEGINNING OF THE QUEUE AS EXPLAINED ON PAGE 17.

THE "MAT READ" INSTRUCTION IS USEFUL FOR SETTING UP
"STATE TABLES" IN PROGRAMS THAT USE SUCH DEVICES : A FULL
EXAMPLE IS INCLUDED ON PAGE 102 .

 THIS INSTRUCTION
DEMANDS COMPLETE
ARRAYS AS INPUT
DATA.

10	DIM	A(3,3)

	1)	2)		
A(1,	1.5	2.6		
A(2,	3.7	4.8		

HERE IS ONE WAY TO FILL A SPECIFIC PART OF AN ARRAY WITH
NUMBERS DEMANDED FROM THE KEYBOARD.

```
200     PRINT "TYPE THE DIMENSIONS"
210     INPUT R,C
220     FOR   I = 1 TO R
230     PRINT "TYPE ROW"; I; "ONE NUMBER PER LINE"
240     FOR   J = 1 TO C
250     INPUT A(I,J)
260     NEXT  J
270     NEXT  I
280     END
RUN
TYPE THE DIMENSIONS
? 2,2
TYPE ROW 1 ONE NUMBER PER LINE
? 1.5
? 2.6
TYPE ROW 2 ONE NUMBER PER LINE
? 3.7
? 4.8
```

THIS COULD BE ACHIEVED IN A DIFFERENT WAY USING THE "MAT INPUT"
INSTRUCTION LIKE THIS :

```
100     PRINT "TYPE THE DIMENSIONS"
110     INPUT R,C
120     PRINT "TYPE"; R; "ROWS OF"; C; "NUMBERS"
130     MAT INPUT A(R,C)
140     END
RUN
TYPE THE DIMENSIONS
? 2,2
TYPE 2 ROWS OF 2 NUMBERS
? 1.5, 2.6
? 3.7, 4.8
```

WHENEVER YOU WANT TO DEMAND DATA FROM THE KEYBOARD IT IS BETTER TO WRITE A SPECIAL INPUT ROUTINE (SUCH AS THAT STARTING AT LINE 200) THAN TO USE THE "MAT INPUT" INSTRUCTION. THREE REASONS ARE:

YOU CAN PRINT HELPFUL INTERMEDIATE MESSAGES SUCH AS THAT ON LINE 230 ~ IMPOSSIBLE USING "MAT INPUT".

YOU MAY TEST THE RANGE OF EACH NUMBER AS TYPED AND TAKE ACTION BEFORE THE WHOLE ARRAY HAS BEEN TYPED. FOR EXAMPLE, IF YOU KNOW THAT ALL NUMBERS SHOULD BE SMALLER THAN ±10:

```
252    IF  ABS(A(I,J)) < 10  THEN  260
254    PRINT "OUT OF RANGE; RETYPE COL."; J
256    GO TO 250
```

THEN YOU COULD INSERT THIS ROUTINE IN THE ROUTINE OPPOSITE.

TYPING ONLY ONE NUMBER PER LINE AVOIDS AN EMBARRASSING PROBLEM: WHAT IF YOU CAN'T GET THE WHOLE ROW ON ONE LINE? SOME BASICS ALLOW AN AMPERSAND ~ & ~ AT THE END OF THE LINE TO SAY "I HAVEN'T FINISHED THE ROW YET": OTHER BASICS OFFER DIFFERENT SOLUTIONS.

SO FOR THE SAKE OF PORTABILITY, IF NOTHING ELSE, DON'T USE "MAT INPUT" FOR DEMANDING DATA FROM THE KEYBOARD. THIS INSTRUCTION IS USEFUL FOR OTHER PURPOSES AS WILL BE SHOWN.

THE LIST FOLLOWING "MAT INPUT" MAY CONTAIN NAMES OF ANY NUMBER OF ARRAYS: ANY OF THESE NAMES MAY HAVE DIMENSIONS AFTER THEM. AS IN THE CASE OF "MAT READ" THE DIMENSIONS MAY BE INTEGERS, VARIABLES OR EXPRESSIONS AS LONG AS THE VALUES EXPRESSED DO NOT EXCEED THOSE IN THE "DIM" STATE-MENTS. IF YOU USE EXPRESSIONS FOR DIMENSIONS MAKE SURE THEY WILL ALWAYS YIELD INTEGRAL RESULTS BECAUSE SOME BASICS USE THE NEAREST INTEGER TO THE RESULT AND OTHERS THE INTEGRAL PART. SOME OTHER IMPLICATIONS OF RE-DIMENSIONING ARE DISCUSSED ON PAGE 79.

```
150    MAT INPUT  A , B(2,1), C(2*X, Y)
```
ALWAYS COMMAS

  THIS INSTRUCTION CAUSES COMPLETE ARRAYS TO BE PRINTED.

```
10    DIM  A(3,3),  B(2,3),  C(2,3)
20    MAT  A = IDN(2,2)
30    MAT  B = CON
40    MAT  C = (-1.5)*B
```

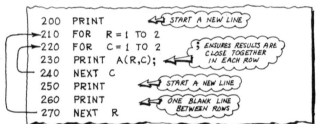

	1)	2)
A(1,	1	0
A(2,	0	1

	1)	2)	3)
B(1,	1	1	1
B(2,	1	1	1

	1)	2)	3)
C(1,	-1.5	-1.5	-1.5
C(2,	-1.5	-1.5	-1.5

HERE IS A ROUTINE TO PRINT THE 2 BY 2 MATRIX STORED IN ARRAY A(,) 〰 AND TO PRINT IT BY ROWS.

```
200    PRINT              START A NEW LINE
210    FOR  R = 1 TO 2
220    FOR  C = 1 TO 2      ; ENSURES RESULTS ARE
                              CLOSE TOGETHER
                              IN EACH ROW
230    PRINT  A(R,C);
240    NEXT  C
250    PRINT              START A NEW LINE
260    PRINT              ONE BLANK LINE
                           BETWEEN ROWS
270    NEXT  R
```

YOU CAN DO THIS WITH A SINGLE "MAT" INSTRUCTION:

```
100    MAT  PRINT   A;     PRINT RESULTS
                            CLOSE TOGETHER
```

AND YOU MAY PRINT ANY NUMBER OF ARRAYS WITH A SINGLE "MAT" INSTRUCTION. THE PUNCTUATION IS EXPLAINED IN MORE DETAIL OPPOSITE.

```
110    MAT  PRINT   A; C,   PRINT C(,)
                             IN ZONES
```

THESE ARRAYS GET PRINTED BY ROWS. (IF YOU WANT *COLUMNS* OF AN ARRAY PRINTED AS ROWS ON THE PAGE USE "MAT B=TRN(A)" FIRST.) THESE ARRAYS ARE PRINTED ACCORDING TO THEIR *CURRENT* DIMENSIONS. THUS ARRAY A(,) WHEN PRINTED WOULD HAVE 2 ROWS WITH 2 NUMBERS IN EACH ROW: IT WAS GIVEN THESE DIMENSIONS ON LINE 20 ABOVE. ARRAY C(,) WOULD HAVE 2 ROWS, EACH OF 3 NUMBERS.

DON'T WRITE DIMENSIONS IN THIS INSTRUCTION. *BASIC KNOWS* THE CURRENT DIMENSIONS OF ALL ARRAYS AND OBJECTS TO BEING REMINDED.

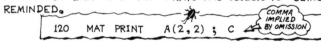

```
120    MAT  PRINT   A(2,2) ; C     COMMA
                                    IMPLIED
                                    BY OMISSION
```

LAYOUT OF THE OUTPUT PAGE FOLLOWS THE RULES GIVEN BELOW ~ THOUGH THERE MAY BE MINOR DIFFERENCES IN SOME *BASICS*.

EVERY ROW OF THE ARRAY STARTS A NEW LINE ON THE OUTPUT PAGE.

THERE IS A BLANK LINE ON THE OUTPUT PAGE AFTER EVERY PRINTED ROW OF THE ARRAY.

IF A ROW OF THE ARRAY DEMANDS MORE THAN THE WIDTH OF THE OUTPUT PAGE (TYPICALLY 72 CHARACTERS) THEN THE ROW IS CONTINUED ON THE NEXT LINE OF THE OUTPUT PAGE.

IF A SEMICOLON FOLLOWS THE NAME OF AN ARRAY IN THE LIST AFTER "MAT PRINT" THEN THE NUMBERS IN EACH ROW ARE PRINTED CLOSE TOGETHER; IF A COMMA FOLLOWS THE NAME THEN THE NUMBERS ARE PRINTED IN ZONES (TYPICALLY 15 CHARACTERS WIDE). THE PRECISE EFFECTS OF SEMICOLONS AND COMMAS IN THIS CONTEXT ARE EXPLAINED ON PAGE 29.

IF THERE IS NO PUNCTUATION AFTER THE FINAL NAME LISTED IN THE "MAT PRINT" INSTRUCTION THEN A COMMA IS IMPLIED BY OMISSION. (PUNCTUATION IS ESSENTIAL *BETWEEN* ITEMS IN THIS LIST.)

YOU MAY FIND THE RIGID FORMAT IMPOSED BY THIS INSTRUCTION GIVES LITTLE SCOPE FOR DESIGNING ATTRACTIVE PAGE LAYOUTS ~ BUT THE INSTRUCTION IS VERY USEFUL WHEN DEVELOPING NEW PROGRAMS.

WITH THE ARRAYS AT THE TOP OF THE OPPOSITE PAGE THE OUTPUT GENERATED BY LINE 110 WOULD LOOK LIKE THIS:

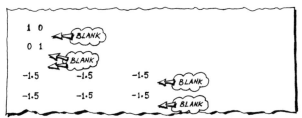

COMPLETE EXAMPLE PROGRAMS

A PROGRAM TO CONVERT **ROMAN** TO MORE FAMILIAR NUMBERS.

THIS EXAMPLE DEMONSTRATES THE USE OF A *SYMBOL-STATE* TABLE ⇔ A STANDARD TOOL IN PROGRAMMING ⇔

ASSUME ALL VALID ROMAN NUMBERS ARE COMPOSED OF THE FOLLOWING ELEMENTS ⇔ NEVER MORE THAN ONE FROM EACH CONSECUTIVE BOX :

THOUSANDS	*HUNDREDS*	*TENS*	*UNITS*
M = 1000	D = 500 DC = 600	L = 50 X = 10 LX = 60	V = 5 I = 1 VI = 6
MM = 2000	C = 100 DCC = 700	XX = 20 LXX = 70	II = 2 VII = 7
MMM = 3000	CC = 200 DCCC = 800	XXX = 30 LXXX = 80	III = 3 VIII = 8
ARBITRARY UPPER LIMIT	CCC = 300 CM = 900	XL = 40 XC = 90	IV = 4 IX = 9
	CD = 400		

《 IT SEEMS CLASSICAL ROME SELDOM USED THE *SUBTRACTIVE* PRINCIPLE INHERENT IN IV , PREFERRING IIII , BUT THIS PROGRAM REFUSES TO HANDLE MORE THAN THREE CONSECUTIVE LETTERS OF THE SAME KIND。》

THE LOGIC OF THE PROGRAM IS CONTAINED IN THE FOLLOWING SYMBOL-STATE TABLE :

					"SYMBOL"			
		M	**D**	**C**	**L**	**X**	**V**	**I**
STARTING STATE →	01	1000 & 02	500 & 03	100 & 09	50 & 05	10 & 10	5 & 07	1 & 11
	02	1000 & 02	500 & 03	100 & 09	50 & 05	10 & 10	5 & 07	1 & 11
	03	ERROR	ERROR	100 & 09	50 & 05	10 & 10	5 & 07	1 & 11
	04	ERROR	ERROR	100 & 04	50 & 05	10 & 10	5 & 07	1 & 11
"STATE"	05	ERROR	ERROR	ERROR	50 & 06	10 & 10	5 & 07	1 & 11
	06	ERROR	ERROR	ERROR	ERROR	10 & 06	5 & 07	1 & 11
	07	ERROR	ERROR	ERROR	ERROR	ERROR	5 & 08	1 & 11
	08	ERROR	ERROR	ERROR	ERROR	ERROR	ERROR	1 & 08
	09	800 & 05	300 & 05	100 & 04	50 & 06	10 & 10	5 & 08	1 & 11
	10	ERROR	ERROR	80 & 07	30 & 07	10 & 06	5 & 08	1 & 11
	11	ERROR	ERROR	ERROR	ERROR	8 & 00	3 & 00	1 & 08

TAKE THE ROMAN NUMBER **CIX** AS AN EXAMPLE : BEGIN WITH A VALUE OF ZERO。 YOU ARE IN *STATE* 01 《 WHERE THE ARROW IS 》 SO LOOK DOWN FROM *SYMBOL* **C** AND FIND 100 & 09 WHICH SAYS "ADD 100 TO THE VALUE & CHANGE *STATE* TO 09"。 SO ADD 100 TO ZERO & MOVE THE ARROW TO 09。 NOW LOOK DOWN FROM *SYMBOL* **I** AND FIND 1 & 11 : SO ADD 1 TO THE VALUE 《100 + 1 = 101》 & MOVE THE ARROW TO *STATE* 11。 FINALLY LOOK DOWN FROM *SYMBOL* **X** AND FIND 8 & 00 : SO ADD 8 TO THE VALUE 《101 + 8 = 109》。 THE 00 MEANS YOU'VE FINISHED。

THE TABLE IS PART OF THE COMPUTER PROGRAM AND PREPARED AS SHOWN BELOW. TO SAVE SPACE EACH ELEMENT OF A(,) IS MADE TO CONTAIN BOTH THE NUMBER TO BE ADDED *AND* THE NUMBER OF THE NEW STATE ⟿ THUS 5 & 07 BECOMES 100 * 5 + 07 = 507. THE ENTRIES SAYING "ERROR" ARE ENTERED AS −1.

```
10   REM      DECODE  ROMAN  NUMERALS
20   DIM      A(11,7),  C$(7)
30   REM   EACH ELEMENT = 100 * ADDITION + NEWSTATE
100  REM        M,      D,      C,      L,    X,   V,   I
110  DATA   100002,  50003,  10009,  5005, 1010, 507, 111
120  DATA   100002,  50003,  10009,  5005, 1010, 507, 111
130  DATA       -1,     -1,  10009,  5005, 1010, 507, 111
140  DATA       -1,     -1,  10004,  5005, 1010, 507, 111
150  DATA       -1,     -1,     -1,  5006, 1010, 507, 111
160  DATA       -1,     -1,     -1,    -1, 1006, 507, 111
170  DATA       -1,     -1,     -1,    -1,   -1, 508, 111
180  DATA       -1,     -1,     -1,    -1,   -1,  -1, 108
190  DATA    80005,  30005,  10004,  5006, 1010, 508, 111
200  DATA       -1,     -1,   8007,  3007, 1006, 508, 111
210  DATA       -1,     -1,     -1,    -1,  800, 300, 108
220  REM
230  MAT READ  A(11,7)
240  DATA   "M",    "D",    "C",    "L",   "X",  "V",  "I"
250  READ   C$(1), C$(2), C$(3), C$(4), C$(5), C$(6), C$(7)
260  REM
```

THE TEXTUAL ARRAY C$( ) IS NOW LIKE THIS:

	C$(1)	C$(2)	C$(3)	C$(4)	C$(5)	C$(6)	C$(7)
	M	D	C	L	X	V	I

IDEALLY WE SHOULD NOW "INPUT" A SINGLE TEXT LIKE "MCDXCII" AND EXTRACT ITS LETTERS ONE BY ONE FOR MATCHING IN ARRAY C$( ). UNFORTUNATELY *BASICS* CAN'T AGREE HOW TO DO IT. SUPPOSE YOU HAD THIS TEXT:

    LET P$ = "FRUSTRATION"

& WANTED TO PUT "RAT" INTO A$: HERE ARE JUST *SOME* WAYS TO DO IT.

    LET A$ = SUBSTR(P$, 6, 3)
    LET A$ = P$(6, 8)
    LET A$ = STR(P$, 6, 3)
    LET A$ = MID(P$, 6%, 3%)
    LET A$ = EXT$(P$, 6, 8)
    LET A$ = P$(:6,3)
    LET A£ = SUB£(P£, 6, 3)

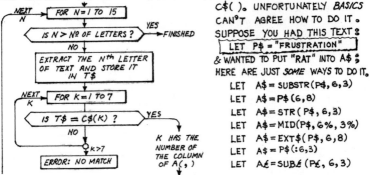

SO WE SHALL BE CONTENT TO "INPUT" LETTERS ONE BY ONE ⟿ SEE OVERLEAF.

ERE IS THE MAIN BODY OF THE PROGRAM FOR DECODING ROMAN NUMERALS:

```
300  REM    MAIN PROGRAM STARTS
310  PRINT "TYPE ROMAN NUMBERS LETTER BY LETTER"
320  PRINT "END NUMBERS WITH *  END RUN WITH **"
330  PRINT "NUMBERS ENDING IV & IX NEED NO *"
340  PRINT
350  PRINT "START"          ← INITIAL "STATE" IN THE TABLE
360  LET R = 1
370  LET M = 0              ← ACCUMULATE RESULT IN M
380  LET C = 0              ← COUNT OCCURRENCES OF IDENTICAL CONSECUTIVE LETTERS
390  LET P = 0              ← "PREVIOUS" LETTER
400  INPUT T$
410  IF T$ = "**" THEN 610      ← END OF RUN
420  IF T$ = "*" THEN 580       ← PRINT ACCUMULATED VALUE IN M
430  FOR K = 1 TO 7
440  IF T$ = C$(K) THEN 480
450  NEXT K
460  PRINT "CRAZY ROMAN NUMBER"
470  GO TO 340              ← NEW START
480  LET X = A(R,K)         ← PICK UP ELEMENT FROM TABLE
490  IF X < 0 THEN 460      ← -1 IN TABLE MEANS ERROR
500  REM  ENSURE ONLY 3 OCCURRENCES OF ANY 1 LETTER
510  LET C = (1 - ABS(SGN(K-P))) * (1+C)   ← IF "PREVIOUS" = "CURRENT" THEN C=C+1 ELSE C=0
520  IF  C > 2 THEN 460
530  LET P = K             ← SET "PREVIOUS" TO "CURRENT"
540  REM  ACCUMULATE RESULT IN M;  CHANGE STATE R
550  LET M = M + INT(X / 100)      ← 1st PART OF ELEMENT
560  LET R = X - 100 * INT(X / 100)   ← 2nd PART = NEW STATE
570  IF  R <> 0 THEN 400    ← INPUT NEXT LETTER
580  REM  PRINT THE RESULT
590  PRINT  M
600  GO TO 340             ← NEW START
610  END

RUN

TYPE ROMAN NUMBERS LETTER BY LETTER
END NUMBERS WITH * END RUN WITH **
NUMBERS ENDING IV & IX NEED NO *
START
? M
? M
? I
? *
 2001
```

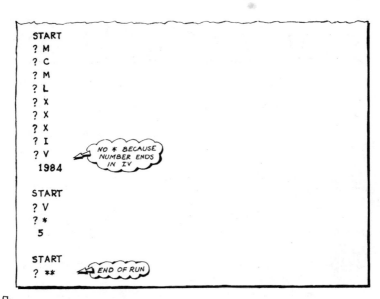

IN THIS EXAMPLE THE FIRST PART OF EACH ELEMENT OF THE
SYMBOL-STATE TABLE IS SIMPLY A NUMBER TO BE ADDED INTO
VARIABLE "M". IN MORE SERIOUS APPLICATIONS THIS WOULD BE
THE LINE NUMBER OF A SUBROUTINE. AFTER PICKING UP AN
ELEMENT (AS AT LINE 480) THERE WOULD BE AN "ON"
INSTRUCTION CAUSING A JUMP TO THE PARTICULAR SUBROUTINE
SELECTED BY THAT ELEMENT. AFTER RETURNING FROM THE
SUBROUTINE THERE WOULD BE AN INSTRUCTION CAUSING A
CHANGE OF STATE JUST AS THAT ON LINE 560.

BEST WAY HOME

A PROBLEM COMMON TO INDUSTRY AND COMMERCE.

HERE IS AN EXAMPLE OF AN "ALGORITHM" ((COMPUTER JARGON FOR "METHOD")) BY WHICH YOU CAN TRACE THE QUICKEST ROUTE THROUGH A NETWORK OF "NODES" AND "EDGES". ((ANOTHER APPLICATION OF THE TECHNIQUE SHOWN IS "CRITICAL-PATH ANALYSIS".)) THIS ALGORITHM WORKS AS LONG AS THERE IS NO MORE THAN ONE EDGE IN ONE DIRECTION BETWEEN ANY TWO NODES.

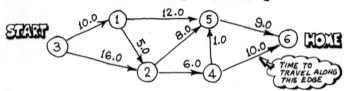

THIS IS HOW IT WORKS. YOU KEEP TRACK OF THINGS AS SHOWN IN THE SKETCH BELOW FOR NODE 2.

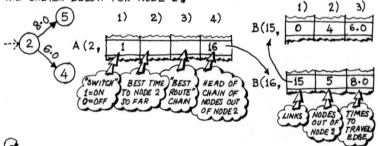

STARTING AT NODE 3 VISIT EACH NODE IN TURN ➡ 3, 4, 5, 6, CONTINUING ROUND AGAIN ➡ 1, 2, 3, 4, 5, 6, 1, 2, etc. UNTIL ALL THE "SWITCHES" ARE "OFF". AT EACH NODE DO THE FOLLOWING ➡ AS DESCRIBED FOR NODE 2:

✰ LOOK AT THE SWITCH IN A(2,1). IF THIS IS "OFF" THEN GO ON TO THE NEXT NODE. IF IT IS "ON" THEN:

✰ PICK UP THE BEST TIME SO FAR: THIS IS IN A(2,2).

✰ USE THE HEAD OF CHAIN IN A(2,4) TO START LOOKING AT ALL NODES RUNNING OUT OF NODE 2. FOR EACH LINK IN THE CHAIN DO THE THINGS DESCRIBED BELOW WITH SPECIFIC REFERENCE TO NODE 5:

✡ PICK UP THE NODE NUMBER (INITIALLY THIS IS 5).

✡ PICK UP THE TIME TO TRAVEL ALONG THE EDGE TO THAT NODE (INITIALLY 8.0) AND ADD THIS TO THE TIME ALREADY PICKED UP FROM A(2,2) TO GIVE T; (THE TIME TO REACH NODE 5 VIA NODE 2).

✡ CONSULT A(5,2) TO SEE IF YOU HAVE JUST FOUND A BETTER ROUTE. IF SO :
- SWITCH "ON" AT A(5,1).
- REPLACE OLD BEST TIME A(5,2) WITH T.
- PUT NODE NUMBER 2 INTO A(5,3) THUS BUILDING A CHAIN THROUGH NODES ON THE BEST ROUTE.

HAVING COMPLETED WORK AT EACH NODE, *SWITCH OFF* THAT NODE.

ARRAYS A(,) & B(,) MUST BE PREPARED BEFORE WORKING ROUND THE NODES AS DESCRIBED ABOVE. ALL THE SWITCHES MUST BE SWITCHED ON, SOME IMPOSSIBLY HIGH JOURNEY TIMES PUT INTO THE SECOND COLUMN OF A(,), AND EVERY NODE MUST BE LINKED TO THE NODES RUNNING OUT OF IT. THE JOURNEY TIME TO THE STARTING NODE MUST BE SET TO ZERO.

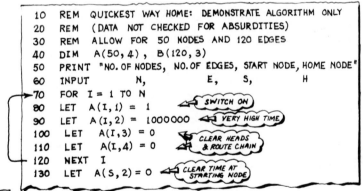

```
10   REM   QUICKEST WAY HOME: DEMONSTRATE ALGORITHM ONLY
20   REM   (DATA NOT CHECKED FOR ABSURDITIES)
30   REM   ALLOW FOR 50 NODES AND 120 EDGES
40   DIM   A(50,4) , B(120,3)
50   PRINT "NO. OF NODES, NO. OF EDGES, START NODE, HOME NODE"
60   INPUT      N,        E,   S,        H
70   FOR I = 1 TO N
80   LET  A(I,1) = 1                    ← SWITCH ON
90   LET  A(I,2) = 1000000              ← VERY HIGH TIME
100  LET  A(I,3) = 0          ← CLEAR HEADS
110  LET  A(I,4) = 0          ← & ROUTE CHAIN
120  NEXT  I
130  LET  A(S,2) = 0   ← CLEAR TIME AT STARTING NODE
```

FOR THE PROBLEM ILLUSTRATED OPPOSITE THE FIRST LINE OF INPUT DATA WOULD BE: ? 6, 9, 3, 6 AND ARRAY A(,) WOULD BECOME:

	1)	2)	3)	4)
A(1,	1	1000000	0	0
A(2,	1	1000000	0	0
A(3,	1	0	0	0
A(4,	1	1000000	0	0
A(5,	1	1000000	0	0
A(6,	1	1000000	0	0

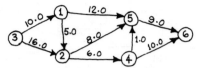

NOW INPUT THE DATA DESCRIBING THE EDGES (IN ANY ORDER) AND LINK EACH FOLLOWING NODE TO THE CHAIN OF ITS PREDECESSOR.

INPUT DATA COULD BE PREPARED AS SHOWN HERE.

NO. OF NODES	NO. OF EDGES	START NODE	HOME NODE
6	9	3	6

EDGES (A) ⟶ (B)		TIME FOR EDGE
3	1	10.0
3	2	16.0
1	2	5.0
1	5	12.0
2	4	6.0
2	5	8.0
5	6	9.0
4	6	10.0
4	5	1.0

```
140   REM  INPUT AND LINK (NO CHECKS ON INPUT DATA)
150   PRINT "A--->---B,  EDGE-TIME"
160   FOR P= 1 TO E
170   INPUT  A,       B,     R
180   LET  B(P,2) = B
190   LET  B(P,3) = R
200   LET  B(P,1) = A(A, 4)
210   LET  A(A,4) = P
220   NEXT  P
```

THE TWO ARRAYS WOULD NOW LOOK LIKE THIS:

	1)	2)	3)	4.)
A(1,	1	1000000	0	Ø̶3̶4
A(2,	1	1000000	0	Ø̶5̶6
A(3,	1	0	0	Ø̶1̶2
A(4,	1	1000000	0	Ø̶8̶9
A(5,	1	1000000	0	Ø̶7
A(6,	1	1000000	0	0

	1)	2)	3)
B(1,	0	1	10.0
B(2,	1	2	16.0
B(3,	0	2	5.0
B(4,	3	5	12.0
B(5,	0	4	6.0
B(6,	5	5	8.0
B(7,	0	6	9.0
B(8,	0	6	10.0
B(9,	8	5	1.0

THE CROSSING OUT IN THE 4TH COLUMN OF A(,) SHOWS HOW THE CHAINS WERE SUCCESSIVELY LINKED.

HERE IS THE MAIN PART OF THE PROGRAM. VARIABLE K COUNTS THE NUMBER OF TIMES NODE 1 IS PASSED WHILST CYCLING THROUGH THE NODES, BUT K IS SET BACK TO ZERO IF A CHANGE IS MADE TO THE ROUTE. THUS WHEN K GETS TO 2 ALL SWITCHES ARE OFF AND THE SOLUTION CAN BE PRINTED.

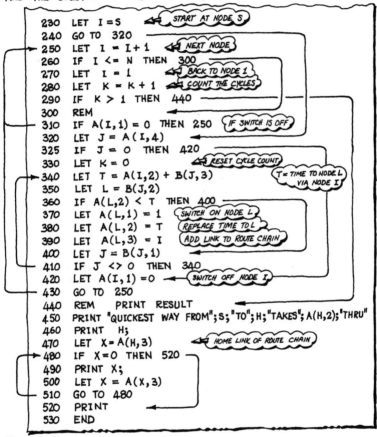

```
230   LET I = S          ◀── START AT NODE S
240   GO TO 320
250   LET I = I + 1       ◀── NEXT NODE
260   IF I <= N THEN 300
270   LET I = 1           ◀── BACK TO NODE 1
280   LET K = K + 1       ◀── COUNT THE CYCLES
290   IF K > 1 THEN 440
300   REM
310   IF A(I,1) = 0 THEN 250    IF SWITCH IS OFF
320   LET J = A(I,4)
325   IF J = 0 THEN 420
330   LET K = 0          ◀── RESET CYCLE COUNT
340   LET T = A(I,2) + B(J,3)    T = TIME TO NODE L VIA NODE I
350   LET L = B(J,2)
360   IF A(L,2) < T THEN 400
370   LET A(L,1) = 1     SWITCH ON NODE L
380   LET A(L,2) = T     REPLACE TIME TO L
390   LET A(L,3) = I     ADD LINK TO ROUTE CHAIN
400   LET J = B(J,1)
410   IF J <> 0 THEN 340
420   LET A(I,1) = 0     ◀── SWITCH OFF NODE I
430   GO TO 250
440   REM    PRINT RESULT
450   PRINT "QUICKEST WAY FROM";S;"TO";H;"TAKES";A(H,2);"THRU"
460   PRINT H;
470   LET X = A(H,3)     ◀── HOME LINK OF ROUTE CHAIN
480   IF X = 0 THEN 520
490   PRINT X;
500   LET X = A(X,3)
510   GO TO 480
520   PRINT
530   END
```

RUNNING THIS PROGRAM WITH THE DATA SHOWN OPPOSITE PRODUCES THE RESULT:

UNITS OF TIME

```
QUICKEST WAY FROM 3 TO 6 TAKES 31 THRU
6 5 4 2 1 3
```

AT THE END OF A RUN THE SECOND COLUMN OF A(,) STORES THE QUICKEST TIMES FROM NODE S TO ALL OTHER NODES IN THE NETWORK.

COMMANDS
AND SIGNING ON

SIGNING ON

CONSULT YOUR USER'S MANUAL — EVERY SYSTEM HAS ITS OWN RULES.

BASIC RUNS ON MINI-COMPUTERS AND MONSTERS ALIKE.

YOU MAY USE A MODERN " DESK-TOP" COMPUTER DESIGNED EXCLUSIVELY FOR DEVELOPING AND RUNNING *BASIC* PROGRAMS.

(SOME OF THESE HAVE KEYS MARKED WITH THE WORDS OF THE LANGUAGE TO SIMPLIFY TYPING. **)**

OR YOU MAY USE ONE OF SEVERAL "TERMINALS" CONNECTED TO A COMPUTER IN THE BUILDING — OR CONNECTED BY TELEPHONE TO A COMPUTER MILES AWAY.

SOME TERMINALS HAVE A KEYBOARD AND VISUAL-DISPLAY SCREEN LIKE A TELEVISION; OTHERS A KEYBOARD AND PRINTING HEAD FOR TYPING ON PAPER.

BIG COMPUTERS OFFER A CHOICE OF LANGUAGE — *BASIC* IS JUST ONE OF THEM. SOMEHOW YOU HAVE TO TELL THE COMPUTER YOU WANT TO USE *BASIC* AS YOU " SIGN ON".

WHEN YOU SWITCH ON A TERMINAL **(** AND, IF IT IS CONNECTED TO A TELEPHONE LINE, DIAL THE NUMBER OF A COMPUTER BUREAU **)** THE FIRST INTELLIGIBLE RESPONSE YOU GET COMES FROM THE COMPUTER'S "OPERATING SYSTEM". YOU THEN HAVE TO TYPE COMMANDS IN A CODE THE OPERATING SYSTEM CAN UNDERSTAND. UNFORTUNATELY THESE CODES ARE TOTALLY DIFFERENT FROM ONE OPERATING SYSTEM TO ANOTHER. SOME HELP YOU BY ASKING QUESTIONS AND SUPPLYING PROMPTS. THE EXAMPLE OPPOSITE CONCERNS AN IMAGINARY SYSTEM SUCH AS THIS BUT YOU WOULD BE LUCKY TO FIND A REAL ONE AS INTELLIGIBLE.

CONVERSATION WITH AN IMAGINARY OPERATING SYSTEM :

```
YOU ARE CONNECTED TO THE "THANATOS" SYSTEM OF
NECROPOLITAN LIFE ASSURANCE INCORPORATED, MORSVILLE.
PLEASE TYPE YOUR ACCOUNT NUMBER
?   123021/6
PASSWORD
?   DAVYJONES
```

MOST SYSTEMS PRINT AND OVERPRINT A BLACK MESS OF CHARACTERS
WHEN ASKING FOR YOUR PASSWORD SO THAT WHAT YOU TYPE ON TOP
OF THE MESS CAN'T BE DECIPHERED BY CURIOUS BYSTANDERS :

```
PASSWORD
?  ▨▨▨▨▨▨▨▨▨

USER 123021 SUBACCOUNT 6 SIGNED ON AT 17.03 HRS
WHAT PROCESSOR OR LANGUAGE
?   BASIC
```

THE CONVERSATION WITH THE OPERATING SYSTEM IS NOT QUITE FINISHED
BUT THIS IS THE POINT AT WHICH SIMPLER OPERATING SYSTEMS (THOSE
FOR COMPUTERS DEDICATED TO *BASIC*) BEGIN WHEN YOU SWITCH ON .

```
NEW PROGRAM OR OLD
?   NEW
GIVE NEW PROGRAM A NAME
?   EXAMPL
```

THE NAME YOU INVENT IS RESTRICTED BY MOST OPERATING SYSTEMS TO
ABOUT SIX LETTERS AND DIGITS OF WHICH THE FIRST MUST ALWAYS BE A
LETTER.

```
BASIC IS READY
```

THIS IS THE POINT AT WHICH MOST EXAMPLES IN THIS BOOK BEGIN
READY TO RECEIVE A NEW PROGRAM TYPED LINE BY LINE PRIOR TO
TYPING "RUN" .

HAVING SIGNED ON, TYPED A PROGRAM AND RUN IT YOU WILL THEN
WANT TO "SIGN OFF". IN MANY SYSTEMS YOU DO THIS BY TYPING
"BYE" OR "GOODBYE" .

```
BYE

USER  123021  SUBACCOUNT 6  SIGNED OFF AT  17.15 HRS.
TIME  CONNECTED = 12 MINS, PROCESSOR TIME = 1.385 SEC.
```

IF YOU GET CONFUSED WHEN CONVERSING WITH AN OPERATING SYSTEM,
TRY TYPING "HELP". SOME SYSTEMS DO RESPOND HELPFULLY : OTHERS
JUST SAY "WHAT?" BUT IT'S WORTH A TRY.

 **COMMANDS**

EACH COMMAND MAKES *BASIC* DO SOMETHING THE MOMENT IT IS TYPED.

THE MOST IMPORTANT COMMAND OF *BASIC* IS "RUN" BUT THERE ARE OTHERS COMMON TO MANY VERSIONS OF *BASIC* AND BRIEFLY DESCRIBED HERE. MOST *BASICS* HAVE USEFUL COMMANDS FOR PROVIDING LINE NUMBERS AUTOMATICALLY, FOR RE-NUMBERING THE LINES OF A PROGRAM, AND FOR JOINING PROGRAMS TOGETHER, BUT THESE COMMANDS VARY TOO MUCH IN DETAIL TO BE INCLUDED IN THIS BOOK. *ALWAYS CONSULT YOUR MANUAL ABOUT THE COMMANDS OF BASIC.*

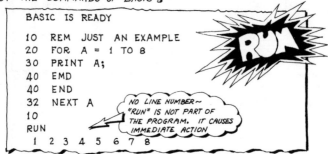

```
BASIC IS READY

10   REM  JUST  AN EXAMPLE
20   FOR  A = 1 TO 8
30   PRINT A;
40   EMD
40   END
32   NEXT A
10
RUN
 1  2  3  4  5  6  7  8
```

NO LINE NUMBER ~ "RUN" IS NOT PART OF THE PROGRAM. IT CAUSES IMMEDIATE ACTION

IF YOU TYPE "RUN" A SECOND TIME YOU WILL GET THE SAME RESULT AGAIN: *BASIC* DOESN'T FORGET A PROGRAM HAVING OBEYED IT.

```
RUN
 1  2  3  4  5  6  7  8
```

IF YOU TYPE "LIST" *BASIC* WILL PRINT A COPY OF THE PROGRAM YOU HAVE TYPED. IT WILL BE A *CLEAN* COPY HAVING BAD LINES REPLACED OR REMOVED AND OUT-OF-SEQUENCE LINES CORRECTLY INSERTED. COMPARE THE ORIGINAL PROGRAM ABOVE WITH THAT BELOW. (SEE ALSO PAGE 7.)

```
LIST
20   FOR  A = 1 TO 8
30   PRINT A;
32   NEXT A
40   END
```

IN SOME *BASICS* TYPING "LIST 30" WOULD CAUSE JUST LINE 30 TO BE PRINTED; IN OTHERS THIS WOULD CAUSE LINE 30 AND ALL SUBSEQUENT LINES TO BE PRINTED. IN SOME *BASICS* TYPING "LIST 20,32" (IN OTHERS "LIST 20-32") CAUSES JUST THAT PART OF THE PROGRAM INCLUDED WITHIN THE STATED RANGE OF LINE NUMBERS TO BE PRINTED.

IF YOU TYPE "SAVE" THEN *BASIC* WILL SAVE IN A "FILE" A COPY OF THE PROGRAM YOU ARE CURRENTLY WORKING ON . THE COMPUTER HAS A *WORKING AREA* (USUALLY IN ITS FAST CORE STORE) AND A *FILES AREA* (USUALLY IN ITS BACKING STORE OF MAGNETIC TAPES AND DISKS). WHEN YOU TYPE "SAVE" A COPY OF THE PROGRAM CURRENTLY IN THE WORKING AREA GOES TO THE FILES AREA . YOU CAN GET IT BACK AGAIN BY TYPING ITS NAME AS DESCRIBED LATER .

```
LIST
20  FOR A = 1 TO 8
30  PRINT  A
32  NEXT  A
40  END
SAVE
```

SENDS A COPY OF THIS PROGRAM TO THE FILES AREA UNDER THE NAME "EXAMPL" — THE NAME GIVEN ON PAGE 113

SEE PAGE 117 ALSO

ONCE IT IS IN THE FILES AREA YOUR PROGRAM WILL NOT DISAPPEAR WHEN YOU SIGN OFF; BUT YOU WILL BE CHARGED RENTAL (USUALLY BY THE DAY) AS LONG AS IT REMAINS IN THE FILES AREA . IT IS ON SUCH RENTALS THAT COMPUTER BUREAUX MAKE THEIR PROFIT .

YOU MAY DISCOVER WHAT YOU HAVE STORED IN THE FILES AREA BY TYPING "CATALOG" (IN BRITAIN YOU MAY TYPE "CATALOGUE"). EVERY SYSTEM PRESENTS THE INFORMATION DIFFERENTLY BUT THE FOLLOWING IS TYPICAL:

```
CATALOG

USER  123021/6    FILES  STORED:

NAME      TYPE            SIZE    DATE CREATED
----      ----            ----    ------------
EXAMPL    SOURCE CODE      1      01 MAR   77
PROG 27   SOURCE CODE      2      28 FEB   77
DATA 65   DATA            27      13 JUN   75
DAT4      DATA            15      24 AUG   72
```

"SOURCE CODE" IS JARGON FOR A PROGRAM IN ITS ORIGINAL FORM — IN THIS CASE *BASIC* .

THE MEANS OF CREATING AND STORING FILES OF *DATA* ARE DESCRIBED ON PAGE 120.

"SIZE" DETERMINES THE DAILY RATE CHARGED FOR RENTAL : THE UNITS OF SIZE MIGHT BE *BLOCKS* OR *TRACKS* OR SOME OTHER MEASURE DEPENDING ON THE KIND OF EQUIPMENT IN USE .

COMMANDS (CONTINUED)

YOU MAY REMOVE A FILE FROM THE FILES AREA ⬡ DESTROY IT COMPLETELY ⬡ BY TYPING "UNSAVE" FOLLOWED BY THE NAME OF THE FILE, OR A LIST OF NAMES SEPARATED BY COMMAS. IN SOME SYSTEMS THE WORD IS "PURGE" ⁏ IN OTHERS "DESTROY".

```
UNSAVE  DATA65 ,  DAT4
```
UNSAVE

IF YOU THEN TYPED "CATALOG" AGAIN YOU WOULD NO LONGER FIND FILES DATA65 OR DAT4 ⬡ AND RENTAL CHARGES FOR THEM WOULD CEASE. IN MANY SYSTEMS YOU CAN MAKE COPIES OF FILES ON PUNCHED PAPER TAPE OR PUNCHED CARDS ⁏ ON SUCH MEDIA YOU CAN STORE FILES WITHOUT PAYING RENTAL YET HAVE THEM READ BACK INTO YOUR FILES AREA WHEN NEEDED AGAIN. THE MEANS OF DOING THESE THINGS VARY GREATLY FROM SYSTEM TO SYSTEM SO CAN'T BE DESCRIBED IN THIS BOOK.

TO BRING A FILE FROM THE FILES AREA TO THE WORKING AREA YOU TYPE THE COMMAND "OLD" FOLLOWED BY THE NAME OF THE FILE WANTED ⁏

```
OLD  PROG27
```
OLD

WHATEVER WAS PREVIOUSLY IN THE WORKING AREA HAS NOW DISAPPEARED, SO REMEMBER TO USE "SAVE" *BEFORE* "OLD" IF YOU WANT TO PRESERVE A COPY OF THE WORKING AREA.

YOU MAY NOW TYPE "LIST" IN ORDER TO SEE A COPY OF PROG27, OR YOU MAY TYPE "RUN" TO EXECUTE PROG27, OR YOU MAY TYPE INSTRUCTIONS IN *BASIC* WHICH WILL ADD TO THE PROGRAM OR REPLACE LINES OF IT. WHEN YOU TYPE "OLD" IT IS EXACTLY AS THOUGH YOU HAD *JUST TYPED* THE PROGRAM NAMED. AND THAT PROGRAM DOES, OF COURSE, REMAIN INTACT IN THE FILES AREA ⁏ THE COMMAND "OLD" TRANSFERS A *COPY* OF THE NAMED PROGRAM TO THE WORKING AREA.

SO WHAT IF YOU ALTER PROG27 IN THE WORKING AREA BY TYPING SEVERAL NEW LINES OF *BASIC* AND THEN TYPE "SAVE" AGAIN ❓ THERE IS ONE PROG27 IN YOUR FILES AREA AND A *DIFFERENT* PROG27 IN YOUR WORKING AREA. THE ANSWER IS THAT *BASIC* PRINTS AN ERROR MESSAGE TO SAY THAT PROG27 IS ALREADY SAVED.

HOWEVER, MOST "SAVE" COMMANDS WOULD ALLOW THIS:

```
SAVE    PROG27A
```

IT SAYS "SAVE THE PROGRAM IN THE WORKING AREA *AS THOUGH IT WERE NAMED PROG27A*". YOUR FILES AREA WOULD NOW CONTAIN BOTH PROG27 AND PROG27A; THE PROGRAM IN THE WORKING AREA WOULD STILL BE CALLED PROG27.

HERE IS ANOTHER SOLUTION TO THE PROBLEM OF DUPLICATED NAMES. THE ILLUSTRATION SHOWS AN INITIAL ABORTIVE ATTEMPT TO FILE TWO PROGRAMS UNDER THE SAME NAME.

```
SAVE
***ERROR***    PROG27 ALREADY SAVED
UNSAVE   PROG27
SAVE
```

IN MOST SYSTEMS THE COMMAND "UNSAVE" WORKS ONLY ON FILES IN THE FILES AREA ∽ NOT ON THE CURRENT FILE IN THE WORKING AREA. IF YOU NOW TYPED "CATALOG" YOU WOULD FIND PROG27 BACK IN THE FILES AREA BUT ITS DATE OF CREATION WOULD BE TODAY'S DATE.

TO CLEAR EVERYTHING OUT OF THE WORKING AREA TYPE THE COMMAND "NEW".

```
NEW
```

IF YOU DON'T DO THIS THEN ANY LINES OF *BASIC* YOU TYPE WILL GO TO CHANGE THE PROGRAM CURRENTLY IN THE WORKING AREA.

NOTICE HOW THE PROCESS OF SIGNING ON ILLUSTRATED ON PAGE 113 *FORCES* THE VERY FIRST COMMAND TO BE:
"OLD" OR "NEW".

8

FILES OF DATA

FILES OF DATA

THE KEYBOARD IS NOT THE ONLY MEANS OF INPUT
NOR IS THE TERMINAL THE ONLY DESTINATION FOR OUTPUT.

SO FAR WE HAVE SEEN THIS:

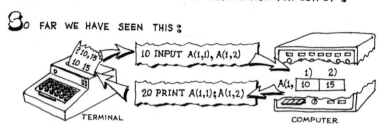

BUT YOU MAY ALSO SEND DATA TO AND FROM A *FILE* IN THE
FILES AREA WHICH IS USUALLY ON MAGNETIC DISK:

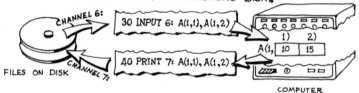

FILES ARE NEEDED MAINLY FOR:

⭐ *COMMUNICATION:* RESULTS OF ONE PROGRAM MAY
BE STORED IN A FILE FOR SUBSEQUENT USE AS
INPUT DATA FOR OTHER PROGRAMS.

⭐ *BACKING STORAGE:* A PROGRAM MAY GENERATE
MORE INTERMEDIATE INFORMATION THAN *BASIC*
CAN HOLD IN THE FORM OF ARRAYS (EVERY SYSTEM
HAS ITS OWN LIMIT ON SIZE OF ARRAY).

TO TRANSFER DATA BETWEEN ARRAYS IN A PROGRAM AND FILES IN
THE FILES AREA USE:

INPUT	(	PAGE	18	)
MAT INPUT	(	PAGE	96	)
PRINT	(	PAGE	28	)
PRINT USING	(	PAGE	34	)
MAT PRINT	(	PAGE	98	)

EXCEPT THAT YOU INSERT A *CHANNEL NUMBER* (FOLLOWED BY A
COLON) AFTER THE WORD "INPUT" OR "PRINT".

HERE IS A SUBROUTINE TO TRANSFER ROWS 1 TO "N" OF ARRAY A(,) TO A FILE ON CHANNEL 7:

```
1000   REM SUBROUTINE TO TRANSFER N ROWS
1010   REM   OF A(,) TO FILE ON CHANNEL 7:
1020   FOR I = 1 TO N
1030   PRINT 7: A(I,1), A(I,2), A(I,3)
1040   NEXT I
1050   RETURN
```

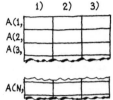

IF YOU "CALLED" THIS SUBROUTINE A SECOND TIME THE NEW CALL WOULD CAUSE MORE ROWS OF NUMBERS TO BE APPENDED TO THE FILE FOLLOWING THOSE TRANSFERRED IN THE PREVIOUS CALL. THUS YOU CAN STORE AN "ARRAY" IN A FILE MANY TIMES LONGER THAN ALLOWED FOR BY THE "DIM" STATEMENT FOR THAT ARRAY.

HERE IS A SUBROUTINE TO INPUT JUST "RECORD R" FROM A FILE ON CHANNEL 6: . WE ASSUME THIS FILE HAS THE SAME STRUCTURE AS THE FILE ON CHANNEL 7: ILLUSTRATED ABOVE. A FILE IS SIMPLY A STREAM OF SINGLE ITEMS; *YOU* HAVE TO ORGANISE ITS STRUCTURE (SUCH AS *ROWS OF THREE* AS "RECORDS" AS IN THIS EXAMPLE).

```
2000   REM SUBROUTINE TO INPUT SINGLE RECORD
2010   REM  "R" INTO B( ) FROM CHANNEL 6:
2020   REM    FIRST RESET FILE TO RECORD 1
2030   RESET  6
2040   REM   WIND THROUGH (R-1) RECORDS
2050   FOR  I = 1 TO R-1
2060   INPUT  6:   A, B, C      "WASTE" R-1 RECORDS
2070   NEXT I
2080   REM   NOW INPUT RECORD R TO B( )
2090   INPUT  6: B(1), B(2), B(3)
2100   RETURN
```

THIS EXAMPLE ILLUSTRATES THE INSTRUCTION "RESET" WHICH IS COMMON TO MANY *BASICS* ALTHOUGH AT LEAST ONE VERSION USES THE WORD "RESTORE" INSTEAD. YOU ARE USUALLY PERMITTED TO RESET SEVERALS CHANNELS BY A SINGLE INSTRUCTION:

```
100   RESET  1, 3, 6
```

THIS INSTRUCTION MOVES A CONCEPTUAL "POINTER" TO THE BEGINNING OF THE FILE ON THE SELECTED CHANNEL SO THAT THE NEXT "INPUT" INSTRUCTION TO BE OBEYED PICKS UP THE FIRST ITEM IN THE FILE. DO NOT USE "RESET" WHILST *PRINTING* A FILE.

FILE NAMES + CHANNELS

WHEN THERE ARE FILES IN A *BASIC* PROGRAM YOU HAVE TO ASSOCIATE *NAMES* OF FILES AS THEY APPEAR IN YOUR "CATALOG" WITH THE *CHANNEL NUMBERS* USED IN "INPUT" AND "PRINT" INSTRUCTIONS. ("CATALOG" IS EXPLAINED ON PAGE 115.) THERE ARE ALMOST AS MANY WAYS OF DOING THIS AS THERE ARE VERSIONS OF *BASIC*. ASSUMING YOU WANT TO INPUT FROM A FILE CALLED "MYDATA" ON CHANNEL 6: AND PRINT A FILE CALLED "RESULT" ON CHANNEL 7: HERE ARE JUST A FEW DIFFERENT WAYS DIFFERENT *BASICS* REQUIRE YOU TO DO IT. (NAMES YOU INVENT ARE USUALLY LIMITED TO ABOUT 6 LETTERS AND DIGITS OF WHICH THE FIRST MUST ALWAYS BE A LETTER.)

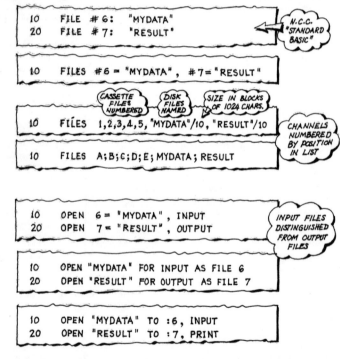

```
10    FILE #6:   "MYDATA"
20    FILE #7:   "RESULT"
```
N.C.C. "STANDARD BASIC"

```
10    FILES #6 = "MYDATA",  #7 = "RESULT"
```

CASSETTE FILES NUMBERED *DISK FILES NAMED* *SIZE IN BLOCKS OF 1024 CHARS.*

```
10    FILES  1,2,3,4,5, "MYDATA"/10, "RESULT"/10
```
CHANNELS NUMBERED BY POSITION IN LIST

```
10    FILES A;B;C;D;E; MYDATA; RESULT
```

```
10    OPEN  6 = "MYDATA", INPUT
20    OPEN  7 = "RESULT", OUTPUT
```
INPUT FILES DISTINGUISHED FROM OUTPUT FILES

```
10    OPEN "MYDATA" FOR INPUT AS FILE 6
20    OPEN "RESULT" FOR OUTPUT AS FILE 7
```

```
10    OPEN "MYDATA" TO :6, INPUT
20    OPEN "RESULT" TO :7, PRINT
```

A FURTHER COMPLICATION IS THAT SEVERAL *BASICS* DEMAND YOU FIRST USE THE "JOB CONTROL LANGUAGE" (*i.e.* THE CODE UNDERSTOOD BY THE COMPUTER'S OPERATING SYSTEM) TO DECLARE AND GIVE DETAILS ABOUT ALL THE FILES YOUR *BASIC* PROGRAM REFERS TO : IN SHORT TO GIVE DETAILS TWICE.

FILES ((CONTINUED))

YOU CAN FILE TEXTS AS WELL AS NUMBERS:

```
100   REM    FILE NAMES AND DATA
110   PRINT 7: "CUSTOMER'S NAME "; N$; S$
120   MAT PRINT 7:  A
```

BUT SOME *BASICS* RESTRICT SUCH MIXTURES OF TEXTS AND NUMBERS TO FILES CODED IN *CHARACTER FORM* AS DEFINED OVERLEAF.

FROM THE PRECEDING EXAMPLES YOU WILL APPRECIATE HOW EASY IT WOULD BE TO PRINT A FILE AND GET IT OUT OF PHASE DURING RE-INPUT: REMEMBER YOU CAN'T *SEE* THE CONTENTS OF A FILE. HERE IS A ROUTINE TO INPUT ON CHANNEL 6: THE FILE PRINTED BY INSTRUCTIONS 100 TO 120 ABOVE ON CHANNEL 7: .

```
200   REM    RE-INPUT CUSTOMER'S NAME & DATA
210   INPUT 6:     M$, Q$
220   MAT INPUT 6:    A
```

BUT THERE IS A HORRIBLE BUG. THE TEXT "CUSTOMER'S NAME " WAS PUT ON THE FILE IN FRONT OF THE CUSTOMER'S TWO NAMES STORED IN N$ AND S$: LINE 210 FAILS TO PICK THIS UP, THUS MAKING S$ INTO THE FIRST ITEM OF MATRIX INPUT WHICH IS RIDICULOUS.

WHEN DEVELOPING PROGRAMS THAT USE FILES IT HELPS TO SEND, SAY, THE FIRST OR LAST ITEM IN EACH TRANSFER TO THE TERMINAL AS A RUNNING CHECK. THE ((CORRECTED)) DEVELOPMENT VERSION OF THE ROUTINE ABOVE BECOMES:

```
200   REM    RE-INPUT CUSTOMER'S NAME & DATA
210   INPUT 6:     T$, M$, Q$
211   PRINT 210; Q$
220   MAT INPUT 6:    A
221   PRINT 220; A(1,1)
```

LINES 211 & 221 JUST FOR DEVELOPMENT

KINDS OF FILE

THERE ARE ESSENTIALLY FOUR KINDS OF FILE: SOME *BASICS* OFFER ONLY ONE KIND, OTHERS MORE. HERE IS A ROUGH ANALYSIS:

(OFTEN CALLED *RANDOM* ACCESS)

IN THE DOMAIN OF FILES THERE IS A "VERTICAL" DIVISION SEPARATING *SEQUENTIAL* FILES FROM *DIRECT ACCESS* FILES.

SEQUENTIAL FILES

EACH FILE HAS A CONCEPTUAL "POINTER" WHICH STARTS AT THE BEGINNING OF THE FILE AND MAY BE SET BACK TO THE BEGINNING AT ANY TIME BY THE INSTRUCTION "RESET".

WHEN YOU SEND INFORMATION TO THE FILE BY THE "PRINT" INSTRUCTION THE NEW INFORMATION GOES ON THE END OF THE FILE AND THE POINTER MOVES ON JUST PAST THE NEW END THUS CREATED.

WHEN YOU INPUT INFORMATION FROM A FILE YOU GET THE INFORMATION POINTED TO. THE POINTER THEN MOVES ALONG TO THE NEXT SET OF INFORMATION READY FOR THE NEXT "INPUT" INSTRUCTION.

OBVIOUSLY, THEN, YOU CAN'T "INPUT" FROM A FILE BEING "PRINTED" UNTIL YOU HAVE FINISHED WITH PRINTING AND "RESET" THE CONCEPTUAL POINTER. IN SOME *BASICS* THIS MEANS CLOSING AN OUTPUT FILE AND OPENING IT AGAIN AS AN INPUT FILE ON THE SAME OR ANOTHER CHANNEL. EXAMPLES ON PREVIOUS PAGES ILLUSTRATE THE USE OF *SEQUENTIAL* FILES.

DIRECT ACCESS FILES

(THESE ARE OFTEN CALLED *RANDOM* ACCESS FILES: A MISNOMER BECAUSE NOBODY WANTS RANDOMLY CHOSEN RECORDS.) WITH DIRECT ACCESS FILES YOU MAY *CONTROL THE POSITION OF THE POINTER*. WHEN THE POINTER IS IN POSITION YOU MAY TREAT THE FILE AS THOUGH IT WERE A SEQUENTIAL FILE. SO *BASICS* THAT PROVIDE DIRECT ACCESS FILES MUST ALSO PROVIDE SPECIAL INSTRUCTIONS FOR MOVING POINTERS TO "RECORD N" AND FUNCTIONS FOR DISCOVERING WHERE THE POINTER HAS GOT TO. DIRECT ACCESS FILES ARE LESS COMMON IN *BASIC* THAN SEQUENTIAL AND ARE NOT FURTHER COVERED HERE.

THERE IS ALSO A "HORIZONTAL" DIVISION OF THE DOMAIN OF FILES SEPARATING *CODED* FILES FROM *BINARY* FILES .

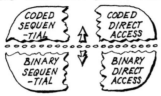

CODED FILES   YOU CAN PRINT THESE AT A TERMINAL OR ON A LINE PRINTER ⇔ EVERY LETTER, DIGIT AND SYMBOL IN THE FILE IS UNIQUELY STORED; USUALLY IN A.S.C.I.I CODE . A PROBLEM WITH CODED FILES IS THAT COMPUTERS USING BINARY ARITHMETIC HAVE TO CONVERT NUMBERS FROM CODED DECIMALS TO BINARY DURING INPUT ⇔ AND FROM BINARY TO CODED DECIMALS DURING OUTPUT . THIS IS WASTED WORK IF YOU DON'T NEED TO PRINT THE FILE AND READ IT: THERE CAN ALSO BE SOME LOSS OF ACCURACY DURING BOTH CONVERSIONS .

BINARY FILES   THESE STORE DATA MORE COMPACTLY THAN IS POSSIBLE WITH CODED FILES AND REQUIRE NO CONVERSION DURING INPUT AND OUTPUT . ON THE OTHER HAND THEY WOULD PRODUCE GIBBERISH IF YOU WERE ABLE TO PRINT THEM AT THE TERMINAL. BINARY FILES ARE STRICTLY FOR STORING INTERMEDIATE RESULTS OF A CALCULATION ⇔ AND READING THEM BACK INTO THE COMPUTER FOR FURTHER COMPUTATION . SEVERAL *BASICS* OFFERING BINARY FILES IN ADDITION TO CODED FILES HAVE DISTINCT INSTRUCTIONS FOR BINARY INPUT AND OUTPUT; TYPICALLY :

> THE WORD "GET" IN PLACE OF "INPUT"
> THE WORD "PUT" IN PLACE OF "PRINT"

AND SOME USE THE WORDS "READ" AND "WRITE" RESPECTIVELY. SOME *BASICS* ALLOW BINARY FILES CONSISTING OF TEXTS . A FEW *BASICS* ALLOW BINARY FILES COMPOSED OF A MIXTURE OF NUMBERS AND TEXTS .

THERE IS NO HOPE OF WRITING COMPLETELY PORTABLE *BASIC* PROGRAMS WHICH USE FILES ⇔ BUT IF YOU STICK TO USING *CODED SEQUENTIAL FILES* YOUR PROGRAM SHOULD NOT NEED MUCH ALTERATION TO MAKE IT RUN ON SOME OTHER INSTALLATION .

SYNTAX

SYNTAX

THIS IS A SUMMARY OF THE SYNTAX — THE WRITTEN FORM— OF *BASIC* AS DESCRIBED IN THIS BOOK. YOUR VERSION PROBABLY DIFFERS, BUT IF IT HAS A DEFINITION OF SYNTAX SET OUT LIKE THIS ONE THEN MOST DIFFERENCES SHOULD BE EASY TO SPOT BY COMPARISON.

A BASTARDIZED "BACKUS-NAUR" NOTATION IS USED FOR THE SUMMARY. MANY SUCH BASTARDS HAVE BEEN CREATED FOR DEFINING THE SYNTAX OF *BASIC* AND SOME ARE VERY AWKWARD TO READ. I HAVE TRIED TO MAKE THIS ONE AS READABLE AS POSSIBLE WITHOUT LOSS OF RIGOUR BUT EVEN SO YOU MAY FIND IT HARD GOING.

SYMBOLS *IN THE DEFINITIONS.*

⇒	SAYS " IS DEFINED TO BE ".
|	SAYS " OR ".
[ ]	SQUARE BRACKETS ENCLOSE ANYTHING THAT MAY APPEAR *ONCE* OR *NOT AT ALL* FOR THE DEFINITION TO HOLD GOOD.
{ }	BRACES ENCLOSE ANYTHING THAT MAY APPEAR *ONCE* OR *SEVERAL TIMES* OR *NOT AT ALL* FOR THE DEFINITION TO HOLD GOOD.

PRINTING STYLES *IN THE DEFINITIONS.*

small letters	ARE USED TO GIVE ENGLISH DESCRIPTIONS WHERE THE MATTER IS OBVIOUS OR WHERE THE SPECIAL NOTATION CAN'T REASONABLY COPE.
CAPITALS (+ −/* ↑) <=:;,.$'"> 012	ARE USED FOR LETTERS, DIGITS AND SYMBOLS WHICH MUST BE COPIED AS THEY STAND TO CREATE A VALID EXAMPLE OF THE THING BEING DEFINED.
Italics	ARE USED TO GIVE NAMES TO THE THINGS BEING DEFINED.

COMMENTS + EXAMPLES.

( ) " SHADOW" BRACKETS ENCLOSE COMMENTS & EXAMPLES WHICH ARE NOT PART OF THE DEFINITIONS.

digit ⇒ one of the digits 0 to 9

letter ⇒ one of the letters A to Z

sign ➔ + | −

operator ⇒ + | − | * | / | ↑   20

separator ⇒ , | ;   28

comparator ⇒ = | < | > | <= | >= | <>   41

text ⇒ " any characters except quotation marks "   12

line ⇒ an integral line number from 1 to 9999   7

function ⇒ SGN | SIN | COS | TAN | ATN | EXP | ABS | LOG | 22, 24

      SQR | INT | RND | FN *letter*

constant ⇒ RND | FN *letter*   25, 26

  ❨ THIS DEFINITION ALLOWS BOTH RND AND RND(X); ALSO FNA & FNA(X) ❩

NEXT THE *COMPOUNDS* ❨ ARBITRARILY DISTINGUISHED FROM *ELEMENTS* ❩ :

integer ⇒ *digit* { *digit* }

❨ e.g. 0 , 012 , 87654 : LENGTH LIMITED BY PARTICULAR VERSION ❩

exponent ⇒ E [*sign*] *integer*

number ➔ *integer* [.] [*integer*] [*exponent*] | . *integer* [*exponent*]   9

❨ e.g. 12 , 12.2 , 12.2E+6 , .12E−6 , 12. , 12.E6 ❩

datum ⇒ [*sign*] *number* | *text*   16

❨ e.g. 2 , −2.5 , "ABC" : AS IN "DATA" STATEMENTS ❩

variable ⇒ *numerical* | *textual*

  numerical ⇒ *letter* [*digit*] | *letter* (*expression* [, *expression*])   10, 60

            ❨ e.g. A, A5, A(4*I), A(I,2*J) ❩

  textual ⇒ *letter* $ [(*expression*)]   ❨ e.g. A$, A$(2+I) ❩   13, 60

lexical ⇒ *text* | *textual*   41

❨ e.g. "ABC" , A$, A$(2+I) : AS IN " IF" STATEMENTS ❩

term ⇒ *number* | *numerical* | *function* (*expression*) | *constant*

    | (*expression*)   ❨ e.g. 6.5 , A(I,J), RND, INT(2+B),(−3*I+J) ❩

expression ➔ [*sign*] *term* { *operator* *term* }   20

❨ e.g. A , + A(I,J) , + A(I, J) * INT (3*A+B) ❩

declaration ➔ *letter* (*integer* [, *integer*]) | *letter* $ (*integer*)   62

❨ e.g. A(4) , A(2,30), A$(26) : AS IN "DIM" STATEMENTS ❩

printable ⇒ *expression* | *lexical* | TAB (*expression*)   28

❨ e.g. A(I,J) * INT(ABS(I+P)) , "ABC" , A$(Q),TAB(X) ❩

adjustment ⇒ (*expression*, *expression*)   79

❨ e.g. (2*A , B(I,J)/6) : AS IN CERTAIN "MAT" INSTRUCTIONS ❩   P.T.O

SYNTAX (CONTINUED)

INDEX

(CONTINUED)

(CONTINUED)

133

INDEX (CONTINUED)